**Praise for *Crosshatch:
the Forgotten Fe...***

What makes, of our lives, a story? What stories are ours to write? These questions pulse across the pages of Crosshatch, a book of history and memoir, research and quest – a book, in other words, of gleaming mirrors. In the able hands of historian Christina Larocco, the feminist Martha Schofield emerges as a complex character, and also a complicated one – a perfect foil for our deeply complicated times and a brilliant companion for Larocco's own most elegant mind.

Beth Kephart,
My Life in Paper: Adventures in Ephemera

Crosshatch is a thoughtful blend of biography and personal essay, and a journey of revisiting well-known US history – this time through the eyes of a woman. Historian Christina Larocco's care for the stories of women, often buried and ignored, is obvious in her treatment of Martha Schofield. Bringing to life the story of this lesser-known feminist in parallel to examining her own personal history, Christina interrogates how the past and present affect each other. Hers is a precise, sharp, and witty voice illuminating that history is made while we live out our everyday lives.

Janna Marlies Maron
Nonfiction Book Coach, Editor & Publisher of
Under the Gum Tree

Crosshatch:
Martha Schofield, the Forgotten
Feminist (1839–1916)

CHRISTINA LAROCCO

A Blackwater Press book

First published in the United States of America by
Blackwater Press, LLC

Copyright © Christina Larocco, 2025

All rights reserved. No part of this publication may be reproduced,
stored in a retrieval system, or transmitted, in any form or by any
means, electronic, mechanical, photocopying, recording or otherwise, without the prior permission of the publishers.

Library of Congress Control Number: 2024952690

ISBN: 978-1-963614-08-4

Cover design by Eilidh Muldoon

Blackwater Press
120 Capitol Street
Charleston, WV 25301
United States

blackwaterpress.com

NOTE ON THE TEXT

Nothing in the sections of this book on Martha Schofield, her life, and her times has been invented. Everything, including Schofield's inner thoughts, has a source. In direct quotations, I have chosen not to use [*sic*] or otherwise indicate imperfect or archaic spelling and grammar, in order to preserve the voices of Schofield and her contemporaries. I have, however, taken two sets of liberties with the sources. First, I have occasionally used my judgment to determine a word or phrase where the handwritten source is difficult or impossible to read. Second, some lines of dialogue, presented in italics here, appear in slightly different forms in the source materials. For example, in Chapter five, Schofield asks her friend Oldden Ridgway, *Why don't thee tell some hair breathed escapes or some soldier's yarn?* The source for this line is a letter between Schofield and another friend. It reads, "one day I said, why dont thee tell some hair breathd escapes or some soldiers yarn."

We cannot bring back to life those whom we find cast ashore in the archives. But this is not a reason to make them suffer a second death. There is only a narrow space in which to develop a story that will neither cancel out nor dissolve these lives, but leave them available so that another day, and elsewhere, another narrative can be built from their enigmatic presence.

— Arlette Farge, *The Allure of the Archives*

Preface

In the summer of 2016, I found Martha Schofield (1839–1916) waiting for me in the Friends Historical Library at Swarthmore College, which brims with hundreds of years' worth of materials documenting the region's Quaker past.

Twenty miles away, Philadelphia, where I live, vibrated with heat. The hottest, worst week coincided with the Democratic National Convention. The Broad Street subway, which took delegates from the Convention Center south to the Wells Fargo Center, was overwhelmed; the bus detoured along mysterious routes that local public transportation seemed determined to keep secret. Mostly I walked to and from work, sweat and friction raising blisters on my feet. On days off I drove out to the suburbs, air conditioner blasting, happy to be away from the heat-radiating city streets.

It was warm even in the archive. This is rare. Usually, archives are frigid. Bring a sweater.

Martha wouldn't have minded the warmth. She had lived in South Carolina for more than fifty years by the time she died. But she wouldn't have minded the cold, either.

If the archives didn't provide refuge from the heat, at least, I thought, they might provide respite from the news – from that long year and, later, the long years that followed, what writer Dayna Tortorici called, in $n+1$, the "long 2016." Living through history seemed strange to me. I was unprepared.

So I decided I would focus on Martha's life, not my own. At the time, I still thought these were different subjects.

* * *

Born into a family of devout Quakers outside of Philadelphia, Martha Schofield dedicated herself to education at an early age, teaching at a school for girls in Purchase, New York, and one for free Black Americans in Philadelphia. She attended women's rights conventions with her mother as early as 1854, and in her thirties and beyond she devoted herself to the women's suffrage movement. She was active in the Philadelphia Female Anti-Slavery Society, raising money and producing handicrafts for fairs. During the Civil War she sewed garments for contraband and volunteered at a local hospital, which took in hundreds of United States soldiers wounded at Gettysburg and elsewhere. During Reconstruction she embarked on what would become her life's work, establishing a school for freed people in Aiken, South Carolina, where she would remain until her death in 1916. She never married or had children, but her relationships with both men and women – relationships she wrote about in intimate detail – were often wrenching. Though she traveled in the same circles as Lucretia Mott, William Lloyd Garrison, and Susan B. Anthony and attained a level of national fame, few today have heard of her.

Once flesh and blood, she exists now only in her papers, mostly letters and diaries. They are detailed almost down to the item in the collection's finding aid, which explains to researchers what they will find in each box and each folder within that box. A finding aid is both a promise and a warning: you will find *this*, but you won't find *that*. Often, especially for women's collections, it issues a version of this disclaimer: "scant information about her personal life." It is very rude of

Fig. 1: Martha Schofield at age twenty-six (1865), when she left for the South, box PA 143, Martha Schofield Papers, RG 5/134, Friends Historical Library of Swarthmore College.

historical figures not to tell us nosy historians what we want to know!

In part, this is because of how women's archives and the field of women's history – my field – have developed. The first generation of women's historians to emerge from second-wave feminism in the 1970s was understandably focused on highlighting extraordinary women's accomplishments, disentangling them from home, family, and the personal or private to show what they had done in the public realms of politics, science, and the arts. This began to change in the last decades of the twentieth century, largely thanks to how those same second-wave feminists, those pioneers of "the personal is political," curated their own papers for donation.

For generations, though, it was only women whose lives adhered to male models of achievement whose papers were deemed worthy of collecting. At the same time, many public women – or their descendants, who were concerned with propriety – purged their records of anything personal. Most famously, reformer Jane Addams burned the letters she exchanged with her longtime partner, Mary Rozet Smith. Writer Louisa May Alcott requested that most of her letters be burned after her death, and her one living sister respected her wishes. Among organizational papers, newspaper clippings, and political statements, it can be very difficult to find anything about subjects' thoughts, feelings, and relationships. Historian Susan Ware had to give up writing a biography of Alice Paul because she could not figure out who the suffragist was as a human being.

But in Martha's case, the promise seemed nearly infinite. She wrote about her thoughts and feelings constantly, providing rare access to a nineteenth-century woman's inner life. I had to know this woman. I had to rescue her from oblivion, from the generations of historians who had not recognized what an astonishing story this was.

Crosshatch

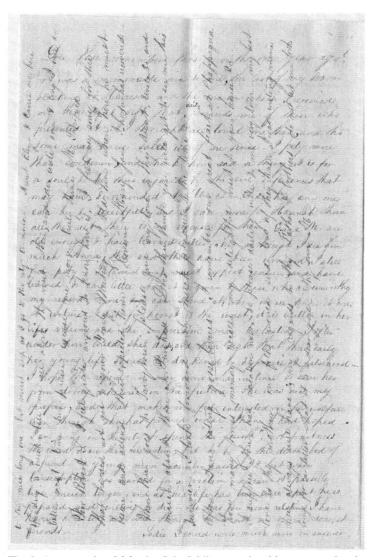

Fig. 2: An example of Martha Schofield's crossed writing, or crosshatch. Schofield to Sadie Brouwer, July 3, 1860, box 1, folder correspondence, 1860, Schofield Papers.

Martha's body was small, barely one hundred pounds; her writing, perhaps to compensate, takes up space. She wanted to be bigger. It's audacious, the insistence on filling up all of those pages. Her letters and diaries took up space wherever she lived, and now they take up six boxes' worth of space in the archive. It's not much compared to some of her male contemporaries, but it's more than most women — first because Martha's race and class afforded her a rare (though circumscribed) leisure to write; second because she did Something Important with her life, and her papers seemed worthier of preservation than did other women's. Even pioneering twentieth-century historian Mary Beard, so essential to the creation of women's archives in the United States, did not think her own papers were worth saving; they revealed, she wrote to an archivist at Smith College, only "the fuzziness of [her] mind."

I began this project with a simple goal: to share the life of a little-known woman from history, and thus to highlight the importance of telling women's stories. Under normal circumstances, it might have remained just that. But the years in which I completed this manuscript, 2016–2021, were no ordinary times. The book turned into something quite different, or something more: a reckoning with my own place in history.

In "A Sketch of the Past," Virginia Woolf distinguishes between the I-then and the I-now: those moments in our writing when we are speaking as our past selves living through a moment, and those when we are looking back and reflecting on an experience.

This is a book about the past, including how the past influences the present: who we are, how we feel, what we believe. But it works the other way around, too: the present — that pesky I-now and her context — also influences the past. Woolf knew this, too. "This past," she wrote, "is much affected by the present moment. What I write today I should not write in a year's time." The present teaches us to understand the past,

Crosshatch

and our relationship to the past, differently.

Both implicitly and at times explicitly, then, this book is about the years in which I wrote it: the age of Trump, which Martha helped me understand and survive; the period in which I grappled, as a white woman, with my own place in history; the era in which, years after I finished my PhD in the subject, I finally started to understand what history *is*; the years in which my own life collapsed and had to be rebuilt.

I call this relationship between the past and the present, between Martha's life and mine, a crosshatch. Crosshatch is a form of nineteenth-century script. Reluctant to waste paper, parsimonious Quaker writers turned their pages and wrote over the initial set of words. The results are intricately beautiful but difficult to read, obfuscating as much as they illuminate. For me, crosshatch also describes a form of storytelling.

This book is a crosshatch, with meaning layered upon meaning, individual lives and historical context woven together. I let my own story peek out from behind someone else's words, someone else's life. "Their voices overlapped in their desperation to tell their stories," writes Liane Moriarty in one of her fictional renderings of women's intertwined lives. Neither of us can wait our turn anymore.[1]

As a girl I created my own crosshatch, intentionally developing handwriting that no one could read, so I could sit in class and write my feelings while still looking like I was paying attention, like I was taking notes. I hid my explosive teen girl emotions in the curlicues of an "s," the loop and swing of a "y," the sweep of an "l" as it rises, twists, and falls. This was the only way I could express myself and still feel safe. Times New Roman, so readable, so revealing, provides no such cover.

This, then, is the only way I know how to write a memoir.

---

1 Liane Moriarty, *The Husband's Secret* (New York: Berkley, 2013), ebook.

CHAPTER ONE: DAUGHTER

As a young girl, Martha and her siblings ran around the hills of Pine Grove, the family farm near Newtown, Bucks County, Pennsylvania. They splashed in Neshaminy Creek, which crisscrossed their farm. Martha played with dolls and dressed in her mother's clothes and marveled over clear glass beads strung together into necklaces.

Martha's mother, Mary Jackson Schofield, had grown up in nearby Darby, where her brother John and other family members still lived. Mary's father, Halliday Jackson, had left his hundred-acre farm equally to his ten children when he died at the age of sixty-five in early 1835, stipulating that any daughters who remained single could make their homes there. Mary was Halliday's favorite daughter, his companion and caretaker since his wife, Jane, had died in late 1830. "Oh my mother! Am I never again to address thee by that tender name?" Mary had written on the occasion. She had watched her mother die. Four years later, Halliday left Mary $200, her first choice of a feather bed, bedding, and a bureau, as well as a silver tankard that had belonged to Jane and a large, new Bible with plates that Jane had designed especially for Mary. Her sisters Elizabeth and Phebe were left to take the furniture Mary did not claim.

Though not especially young at thirty-five, Mary was a

new wife when Halliday died. She and Oliver had married just two months earlier, and she was pregnant with twins, Sallie and Lydia, born later that year. Martha, born in 1839, was named for Oliver's mother.[1]

Mary was a well-known speaker and minister, delivering sermons on abolitionism to Friends as far away as Virginia. While Mary was away, Oliver reported on the children. "Mart has been very good, the rest middling," he wrote to her around 1840, though I'm sure Martha could be a scamp as well. With Oliver's encouragement, Mary continued her ministry as her husband's health deteriorated in the early 1850s. His death in 1852 was not a surprise, and he had done all he could to prepare the children for life without him.[2]

After Oliver's death, Mary moved the family to Byberry and then to Darby. Delaware County, where Darby is located, curves around the state of Delaware to hug the western border of Philadelphia. When European settlers first arrived in the area, fowl and deer were plentiful, and pigeons darkened the sky. It is a hilly country, crisscrossed by streams that empty into the Delaware River, over the millennia cutting hills and valleys into the landscape and providing a source of power, fertile ground for farming, and fish for catching. When glaciers crept across the earth, they brought to the region a layer of gravel, sand, and clay, mineral deposits that enriched the soil. In the nineteenth century, "almost every country house … [was] supplied from a never-failing spring of pure,

---

1 [Mary Jackson Schofield], "Written 1st Month 1831 in a Season of Mournful Meditation," [Jan. 1831], Martha Schofield Papers, Friends Historical Library, Swarthmore College, Swarthmore, PA (all manuscript sources from this collection unless otherwise noted). Much of the collection is now digitized and is available here: https://archives.tricolib.brynmawr.edu/resources/5134scho.

2 Oliver Schofield to Mary Jackson Schofield, n.d. [ca. 1840], quoted in *Katherine Smedley, Martha Schofield and the Re-Education of the South, 1839–1916* (Lewiston, NY: Edwin Mellen Press, 1987), 12.

Fig. 3: Martha Schofield as a child, *Scattered Seeds*, Tenth Month (October), 1916, box 1, folder n.d., Schofield Papers.

Fig. 4: Katharine W. Hanes, "'Pine Grove' – Martha's Birthplace," in Mary S. Patterson, *Martha Schofield (1839–1916): Servant of the Least* (1944), unnumbered page.

Fig. 5: View on the Neshaminy watercolor [view 2], undated, Historical Society of Pennsylvania medium graphics collection (Collection V64), HSP.

soft water, and nearly all the fields of every farm have running springs through them ... No one who has ever seen the charming scenery of this part of the State can exclude from the recollection of it the well-tilled farms, with their tastefully-planned homes, capacious barns, fields of waving grain, and the herds of cows that supply milk and butter of the very best quality to the Philadelphia market."[3]

Mary and the children joined the Darby Friends Meeting, which dated back to 1684, when it met in the home of abolitionist John Blunston. In 1805, the meeting moved to the structure that still stands today, built from stones from local quarries – peculiar stones, stones that geologists believe were among the earliest to form as the earth cooled but that were never submerged in water, some that had been injected with molten liquid rock, melted, and recrystallized around the injection site. Over a century later, Martha would be buried outside of that old building with the strange stones.

* * *

Martha had history in her blood. Her maternal ancestor Ralph Jackson was burned at the stake in Stratford during the reign of Mary I, a Catholic, eight years before Shakespeare was born, in 1556. "The blood in my veins runs back to 1556 when one of my ancestors was burned at the stake because he wanted to serve God in his own way," Martha recalled at the end of her life. In the next century, her fifth great-grandmother, Margaret Fell, became one of the founders of Quakerism. Fell spent years in prison for her beliefs, using the time to write tracts and pamphlets. One of them was *Womens Speaking Justified* (1666), in which she argued that

---

3 Henry Graham Ashmead, *History of Delaware County, Pennsylvania* (Philadelphia: L. H. Everts & Co., 1884), 212, 213; Ellwood Harvey, "Physical Geography and Geology of Delaware County," in Ashmead, 1.

Crosshatch

human society, not God or the Bible, placed restrictions on women's lives. "God hath put no such difference between the Male and Female as men would make," Fell wrote.[4]

Ancestors on both sides of Martha's family were among the Quaker faith's earliest followers. Brothers Anthony and Richard Jackson founded the first Quaker meeting in Ireland, though in doing so they risked arrest. Jonathan Schofield, her father's great-grandfather, migrated to Pennsylvania in the eighteenth century.

When Martha left home at the beginning of October 1865, compelled by a calling to teach formerly enslaved individuals, she drew on family tradition. She had been planning her move since at least 1862. "In the secret of my being," she recalled decades later, "I had promised my life to the Masters Service, and only waiting my ideal Mothers consent – which she gave later." Even at twenty-six, she needed her mother's permission to go so far.[5]

It had not been easy to procure. When Martha first raised the idea of teaching in the South, Mary forbade it. But faith made her relent.

In the week after Martha left, the house seemed empty to Mary. Several times each night, she got up from bed, went to the window, and looked out at the moon, wondering where Martha was, if she was happy. During the day, she sought items in the house that reminded her of Martha, cleaned Martha's room, fretted over whether Martha had brought adequate bedding, berated herself for not having thought of it sooner. Put up new wallpaper in the house. Copied by hand all of the letters that Martha wrote while she was away,

---

4 MS draft letter to Governor Coleman Livingston Blease, 1912; Margaret Fell, *Womens Speaking Justified, Proved and Allowed of by the Scriptures, All such as speak by the Spirit and Power of the Lord Jesus* (London, 1666), 2.

5 MS, handwritten note, in *In Memoriam*, p. 43, ed. Anna Webster Bunting et al. (Philadelphia: Friends' Book Association of Philadelphia, n.d. [1906?]).

collecting them in one book where they would always be together. This busywork didn't keep away the bigger worries, but it helped.

Just before she left, Martha placed a note in Mary's dresser drawer. *Do not mourn me. Do not be anxious about me. I am doing my duty. I hope to return.*[6]

The historian knows what Martha and Mary did not: save for brief visits, Martha never did return home. I wonder if Martha *did* know this. When she applied to teach for the Pennsylvania Freedmen's Relief Association, she asked to be sent as far south as possible. From 1865 until her death in 1916, home was South Carolina.

* * *

For years, I wondered why Martha left. There was duty of course, and a genuine desire to do good and be useful. But was that enough? Being away seemed to break her heart. I found the answer in a note scribbled in 1910, long after such personal confessions usually appeared in Martha's writing. One night in the early 1860s Martha knelt down and made a bargain with God: she would devote her life to his service if he would grant happiness to her two dearest friends, Sadie Brouwer and John Bunting. She would sacrifice herself for them.

God doesn't seem to have lived up to his side of the bargain. Sadie didn't live to see forty; in 1910 she had been dead for over thirty years. John lived into his sixties but never found an outlet for his creative talents.

> Do not wonder why none of the poetry of our youthful days flows from my pen − ," he wrote to Martha in 1869, "do not think it is because I will not trust thee

6 MS to Mary H. Child, Oct. 5, 1865 (copy).

> — I really never have time to write them down & little very little time to <u>think</u> them — I know however that, choked down as they have been, & crushed under the heavy wheels of business, which keep turning, turning, turning, until my head turns with them, they are still <u>there</u> ... Old memories, when I am alone even for a few moments, precious divine harmonies which sometimes gush out from the musical performances that I listen to, a thought of peculiar tenderness, or the sight of a child's innocent face will often moisten my eyelids & make my heart beat quick — .[7]

If Martha realized this, she would only blame herself. Her sacrifice must not have been enough. Perhaps it would have been no different if she had stayed.

Would staying have made Mary happy? Martha always worried that she was a disappointment to her mother, that she had been bad, not good at all. This is what she spent her thirtieth birthday thinking about. "<u>Thirty years ago</u>," she wrote in her diary that day, "my dear Mother gave me her first kiss, — 30 years — has my life been an honor and a joy to her, have I proved a worthy daughter to so true and noble a Mother — . Alas! Alas — I fear there has been many many errors, and little to be proud of — ."[8]

Perhaps a daughter can only disappoint, in a world that doesn't let her be her full self.

---

7 MS diary, May 11, 1869
8 MS diary, Feb. 1, 1869.

CHAPTER TWO: STUDENT

In the mid-nineteenth century, the Schofields were among the tiny handful of radical white abolitionists in the nation. They worked and socialized with members of Philadelphia's Black elite, including Frances Ellen Watkins Harper and members of the Forten–Purvis family. Harriet Purvis, granddaughter of abolitionist titan James Forten and daughter of Robert Purvis and Harriet Forten Purvis, cofounder of the Philadelphia Female Anti-Slavery Society, was exactly Martha's age, and as young women the two were friends. As a little girl, Martha's mother took her to see William Lloyd Garrison. "He laid his hand on my head & <u>blessed</u> me," she remembered decades later.

The Schofields' farm was a stop on the Underground Railroad, and Martha's parents, Mary and Oliver, were conductors. Refugees from the South gathered around the fire in the kitchen, where the children listened to their stories. Oliver brought the refugees to the next station under cover of night. Even among Quakers, the Schofields were radical. In 1848, members of the Makefield Monthly meeting had threatened to disown Oliver based on unrelated charges, but Mary believed it was punishment for his outspoken commitment to racial equality.

The Schofield household also included, at various times,

young Black women and men employed as laborers. In 1850, fifteen-year-old Levi Johnston, who had likely been born free in Maryland, and thirteen-year-old Elizabeth Kennie, who had lived all her life in the free state of Pennsylvania, lived with the Schofields. Ten years later, Elizabeth Johnson, a fifteen-year-old, Pennsylvania-born seamstress, lived with Martha's family. I wonder if they spotted the refugees, if the refugees spotted them. What would they have said to each other? Their lives were so different, but they could in an instant have been rendered the same.

One night in October 1851, twelve-year-old Martha tiptoed into the living room clad in a nightgown, her hair tumbling down her back. She knelt at the feet of her mother, Mary, who read her Bible by candlelight.

I was asleep, Martha told Mary, *but I was awakened by some strange noises so I got up and looked out of the window.* There she espied her father hitching a horse and buggy and driving away with an unknown woman, a stranger wearing Mary's clothes.

Thee has heard thy father tell what a slave is, hasn't thee? Mary asked.

Yes.

The woman had escaped and was headed for Canada, though even in the free state of Pennsylvania she had to disguise herself as a white woman to evade mercenaries.

Are all the slaves running away? Martha asked.

No, dear, because there are thousands of them. By 1860, there were four million.

In another version of this story, Laura Duncan appeared in the Schofields' kitchen in 1857 and collapsed into a chair, out of breath. The thirty-year-old light-skinned Black woman had barely escaped from the posse of white men, some of them officers of the law, and hunting dogs that had chased her for over a week.

Who can thee be? Who can thee be? — and what does thee want here? Mary asked, running into the room in surprise. Haltingly, Laura explained that she was running for Canada. Her lash-scarred back, broken bones, and head gash suggested the physical abuse she had suffered, but not the psychological anguish. One month earlier, her husband, Jim, ten-year-old son, Gabe, and daughter, Jennie, had each been sold to different slavers in different states. Laura did not believe she would ever see any of them again.

Martha, Mary addressed her eighteen-year-old daughter, *do thee find thy father at once and tell him to come to the house as quickly as possible.* Martha held an apron in front of her face to hide her tears, then ran to get her father. She and her mother dressed Laura in an old shawl and bonnet of Mary's, and Oliver and Laura drove north with haste. Within thirty minutes, the search party arrived at the Schofield's home, which they tore apart in search of the refugee. Only several days after his departure did Oliver feel that he had gone far enough to ensure Laura's safety.

It hardly matters whether these accounts — one written by Martha's grandniece, one by an admiring former student and protégé, both memorializing Martha after her death — represent the literal truth. The incident formed an important part of Martha's origin story, her understanding of where she came from, who her people were, and what her mission was.[1]

The only encounter that Martha recorded in her own hand came in 1860, when Martha was twenty-one and the

---

1 The two accounts are *Elisabeth Jenkins Dresser, Scenes in the Life of Martha Schofield*; and Matilda Evans, Martha Schofield, *Pioneer Negro Educator: Historical and Philosophical Review of Reconstruction Period of South Carolina* (Columbia, SC: DuPre Printing Company, 1916), 5–8. Dresser was the granddaughter of Martha's sister Sally. Matilda Evans, who attended the Woman's Medical College in Philadelphia and became the first Black woman licensed to practice medicine in South Carolina, was the best-known graduate of the Schofield School.

nation was just months from war, and a young man appeared at the door. "This morning, my heart was made deeply sad by the sight of a poor human soul seeking to find the free soil of Canada," Martha wrote in her diary. She and her family fed the young man, gave him a new set of clothes to wear, and pointed him north. "The earnest prayer of my heart is that he will find a free home."[2]

* * *

All of the Schofield children were aware to some degree of the southern refugees and their parents' participation in the network that aided them. It was a regular enough occurrence. Eliza, the youngest, was just fourteen when she recorded another incident, which she may have learned about from Harriet Forten Purvis:

> Last night about 8 o'c two men and a constable drove up to a house over in Babylon went in and seized a man by the name of Eric Wright draged him out and put him in a carriage and drove rapidly away before any body had time to go to his assistance. When they seized him his poor wife was so much frightened that she threw her arms around him to hold him crying as loud as she could Kidnappers Kidnappers, when the constable coldly took a pistol from his pocket put it to her head and told her if she did not let go he would shoot her on the spot. They took him right to jail the next day Robt Purvis & Henry Bowman went and saw him; the constable said he was a fugitive from Justice … But they ought not to have taken him in the way they did without showing their warrant and doing as they did. He was betrayed by his brother-in-law who went

2 MS diary, Aug. 10, 1860.

Crosshatch

to his house the 6th day pretending and then went and betrayed him.[3]

Though a free state, Pennsylvania was not safe for individuals who had escaped from slavery, as federal law required — and financial reward incentivized — residents to turn in these sojourners. The Schofields would not do so, of course, but such integrity was not without consequences. Thomas Garrett and John Hunn, white Underground Railroad agents in the slave state of Delaware, were driven nearly bankrupt by fines and prosecutions resulting from their violations of the Fugitive Slave Act. Less scrupulous Northerners, moreover, clamored for the rewards. Along the border between Pennsylvania and Delaware near the Schofields' home, the owner of a pub named the Practical Farmer kept a constant lookout for fugitives, hoping for a reward.

Still, the border between these states (and between Pennsylvania and Maryland, another slave state) was far from meaningless. At the nexus of the three, freedom and slavery were so close, abolitionist Frederick Douglass observed, that at times it seemed absurd to consider the journey an arduous one. But danger lay at the borders. "The nearer the lines of a slave state to the borders of a free state," Douglass noted, "the greater was the trouble." Hired slave catchers patrolled these areas with a vigilance unmatched elsewhere, even making forays into parts of free states that lay near borders with slave states. "The border lines between slavery and freedom were the dangerous ones, for the fugitives. The heart of no fox or deer, with hungry hounds on his trail, in full chase, could have beaten more anxiously or noisily than did mine, from the time I left Baltimore till I reached Philadelphia," Douglass recalled. Wilmington, Delaware, was the "last point of imminent danger, and the one I feared most" — the final obstacle

3 Eliza Schofield diary, 1st day 17th [Sept. 17, 1854].

between the great activist and intellectual and the "Quaker City," between slavery and freedom. Douglass's compatriot Harriet Tubman also traveled through Maryland and Delaware to Pennsylvania. As she recalled years later, "when I found I had crossed that line, I looked at my hands to see if I was the same person. There was such a glory over everything; the sun came like gold through the trees, and over the fields, and I felt like I was in Heaven."[4]

* * *

Sharon Boarding School, which Martha's uncle John and aunt Rachel Jackson had founded in 1837, was another stop on the Underground Railroad. It wasn't just in their abolitionism that Martha's friends and family were radical. Established to instill Quaker values in girls in a setting as academically rigorous as boys' schools, Sharon also exemplified the Quaker commitment to gender equality. "Experience having amply show that the same instrumentalities which are adapted to promote the education of boys," school administrators argued, "are equally well suited to develop the minds of girls, the proprietors of this Female Seminary have endeavored to furnish it with all the aids to instruction in the various branches of science and literature usually employed in the higher seminaries of learning for the other sex." Sharon was one of several schools, including the Westtown School, founded in 1799 in West Chester, and Kimberton, founded in 1818 near Norristown, established in southeastern Pennsylvania and northern Delaware in the late eighteenth and early nineteenth centuries to educate young Quakers – espe-

---

4 Frederick Douglass, *Life and Times of Frederick Douglass* (Hartford, CT: Park Publishing Co., 1882), 198–99, 248, 249; Harriet Tubman quoted in Sarah H. Bradford, *Scenes in the Life of Harriet Tubman* (Auburn, NY: W. J. Moses, 1869), 19.

cially or exclusively young Quaker women. Westtown, Kimberton, and Sharon trained the next generation of "Quaker teaching daughters," those whose reform work often revolved around education and for whom teaching provided economic independence. Of these, Sharon sounds the most utopian. Martha and her sisters spent several years there: Sallie and Lydia attended starting in 1848; three and a half years younger, Martha joined them there by 1852, when she was thirteen. The youngest sister, Eliza, attended from 1854–56.[5]

Sharon was located on the farm that Halliday Jackson had willed to his children. Thanks in part to the continuing growth of nearby Philadelphia, the Jacksons' farm turned a consistent profit, allowing John and Rachel to pay the school's teachers and the farm's superintendent, George S. Truman, keep tuition as low as possible – $80 per twenty-week term in 1852 – and maintain a modest but stable lifestyle for themselves.

The three-story building itself was an immense, imposing structure, Quaker-plain and unornamented save for a large, domed observatory. The lawns and gardens relieved its stark architecture, "showing," as one observer put it, "that the owner was not the victim of any sectarian prejudices, but worshipped *toward* the Spirit of Universal Beauty. Students promenaded on the grounds in the afternoon, arm-in-arm with each other or their teachers. Inside it was well-lit with gas, with open stairways and ample windows. Classes were held in the large, open lecture room and adjoining laboratory, where specimen- and instrument-filled glass cases lined the walls.[6]

Some one hundred girls lived in the school's quarters;

5 Joan M. Jensen, "Not Only Ours but Others: The Quaker Teaching Daughters of the Mid-Atlantic, 1790–1850," *History of Education Quarterly* 24, no. 1 (1984): 3–19.

6 Elizabeth Lloyd, "Worthy Friends of the Nineteenth Century. – III. John Jackson." *Friends' Intelligencer*, May 16, 1903.

Fig. 6: E. W. Thomas, View of Sharon Boarding School, ca. 1840. Courtesy of the Free Library of Philadelphia, Print and Picture Collection.

Crosshatch

three large rooms filled with double beds. Their days were full, beginning with a 5 or 6 a.m. wake-up call. They attended classes, walked to the meetinghouse a mile distant two times a week, and performed their assigned chores, including sewing, sweeping, serving meals, and distributing laundry. At night, with the gas lights snuffed out, the girls were left alone to whisper, laugh, and play tricks, the last two forbidden by strict Quaker virtues but punished only by gentle warnings.

John and Rachel Jackson hoped to educate a cohort of women capable of thinking for and supporting themselves. In 1849, Rachel argued that "the office of the educator is not to crowd the mind with word and facts, but to stimulate it to vigorous action."[7] Sallie and Lydia would have heard Rachel exhort students in 1849 not to let themselves become dependent on men:

> We are sometimes called the weaker sex; and is it not because we trifle away our time and talents upon objects unworthy of a dignified mind? As the plant, which is strong and vigorous in its native situation becomes a dependent vine when tied to a frame, so too many of our sex are the mere helpless dependents on the energies of brothers, fathers, and husbands.[8]

The role of women was also a perennial topic in students' weekly debates. "Our subject for debate last time and the time and the time before was 'does women occupy the sphere she was designed to fill' what is thy opinion on the subject," student Lib Cranston wrote to her friend Hannah F. Wilson, a former Sharon student and Martha's first cousin,

---

7 [Rachel Jackson], *Address to the Pupils of Sharon Boarding School, by the Female Principal. At the Close of the Session 1849.* (Philadelphia: T. E. Chapman, 1849), 7.

8 Jackson, Address to the Pupils of Sharon Boarding School, 4.

in 1853. Martha may have participated in at least some of these debates. An unsigned, undated manuscript in Martha's papers, possibly written for just such a debate, argued that women should submit to their husbands. "As a matter of fact, the woman's power, is not equal to the man's; the men generally believe, this is right. I think it is right." Did Martha write this piece? The handwriting certainly resembles hers.[9]

Sharon students received instruction in the usual subjects, including English language and grammar, mathematics, and, more than any other, science. Chemistry experiments in the laboratory, botanical study in the fields, *papier maché* models of the human body in the biology classroom. Students learned geology, the eons over which mineral deposits and layers of rock accreted.

More unusual: fellow Quaker Ann Preston, first dean of the Woman's Medical College of Philadelphia, lectured Sharon students on physiology. Preston was also the graduate of a Quaker boarding school, and in 1850 she expounded on the joys of learning: "It is a glorious thought … We may not sit down in dumb despair, we may read, think, discipline ourselves by daily study, find our reward in an ever widening vision." Teaching physiology to girls, however, was a radical undertaking, and at first "several of the parents were somewhat shocked at the idea of having a model of a woman's form exhibited to the pupils and even taken to pieces before their very eyes." But Preston presented the material so circumspectly that these fears were quelled. Even the far more radical Mary Gove Nichols remained circumspect in her lectures to women, focusing, as did Preston, on the evils of corsets and other restrictive appurtenances.[10]

9 Lib Cranston to Hannah F. Wilson, Dec. 5, 1853, in *Dear Hannah: A Collection of Letters Depicting Quaker Life in Rural Philadelphia, Pennsylvania, 1850–1860*, ed. C. B. Frederick (JEAM Norwey Publishing, 2011); "Essay on Women's Rights," n.d., Schofield Papers.

10 Ann Preston to Hannah Darlington, Feb. 9, 1850, quoted in Jensen,

Surely Preston infused her lectures with her characteristic feminism. In 1852, she gave the keynote speech at a women's rights convention held in West Chester, the first of its kind in Pennsylvania. "We ask," she pleaded, "that woman shall be trained to unfold her whole nature; to exercise all her powers and faculties ... All women are not wives and mothers, but all have spirits needing development, powers that grow with their exercise." Of the four Schofield sisters, only one married.[11]

What did these girls, young adolescents, think as they listened to Preston's lectures? Did they ask questions about menstruation, about desire? Among women, it would have been all right for Preston to discuss an issue that male doctors largely considered an ailment at best and a scourge at worst. Likely many of the young women in Preston's audience bled as they listened. A few may have done so freely, depending on layers of clothing to hide the flow. But more of these middle-class women would have worn T-bandages – napkins tied around their hips with string or ribbon – perhaps going through a dozen per day. Perhaps fifteen. Perhaps twenty, all of which needed to be changed, and stored somewhere on their person during the day, and washed. A few may have used homemade tampons or other technologies. Medical literature recommended specific solutions, but more often women improvised with their own distinctive devices and palliatives, shared with family and friends in recipe books.

* * *

Astronomy was John's special passion, the Sharon observa-

"Not Only Ours but Others," 17; Lloyd, "Worthy Friends of the Nineteenth Century. – III. John Jackson." May 16, 1903.

11 Ann Preston speech, June 3, 1852, in *The Proceedings of the Woman's Rights Convention, Held at West Chester, Pa., June 2d and 3d, 1852* (Philadelphia: Merrihew and Thompson, 1852), 24–25.

tory – complete with over $4,000 worth of equipment – his pride and joy; "he worshipped ... constantly in 'the temple whose dome is the sky.'" At night, girls traipsed to the top of the house to gaze at the stars, taking turns with the school's state-of-the-art telescope, which cost $1,733 and which school circulars described in poetic detail. "No subject has supplied subject matter so interesting to the contemplative mind of man, as the structure of the universe," wrote English astronomer William Pearson in 1824, and John seemed to agree.[12]

As these girl-scientists gazed into the universe, they may have remembered the poem Rachel once read to them, "To the Ursa Major," by Henry Ware Jr.:

> ... Take the glass
> And search the skies. The opening skies pour down
> Upon your gaze thick showers of sparkling fire;
> Stars, crowded, throng'd, in regions so remote,
> That their swift beams – the swiftest things that be –
> Have travell'd centuries on their flight to earth.[13]

Roughly eighty light years from the sun, the stars in the Ursa Major, or Big Dipper, asterism are our relative neighbors. Their light had taken decades, not centuries, to reach the earth. Light that left these stars in the year that Martha died shone over my adolescence. Stars "can see in the future," Martha once wrote in a different context. Looking through the telescope, the girls saw messages from the past, incomplete guides to what was. They must have felt so small, girls

---

12 Lloyd, "Worthy Friends of the Nineteenth Century. – III. John Jackson." May 16, 1903; Sharon Female Seminary, Circular of the School, 9.

13 Henry Ware Jr., "To the Ursa Major," in The Works of Henry Ware, Jr., D.D.: Miscellaneous Writings, vol. 1, ed. Chandler Robbins (Boston: James Munroe and Company, 1846), 113. Jackson read students portions of the poem in 1849. Jackson, Address to the Pupils of Sharon Boarding School, by the Female Principal, 11.

in a world that wasn't made for them. They were far from the center of the universe. But Sharon also made them, and their world, bigger. "I began to live here," one student remembered. And perhaps, as they learned about Galileo, they thought about how scientific change was like social change, the slow, halting process by which people abandon their old beliefs – about stars, about women, about slavery.[14]

---

14 Lloyd, "Worthy Friends of the Nineteenth Century. – III. John Jackson." May 16, 1903; MS to SB, Fall 1861.

INTERLUDE: (THIS) PROVINCIAL LIFE

My childhood was nearly as bucolic as Martha's. White Clay Creek runs just east of my childhood home, where the corners of three mid-Atlantic states come together; following surveyor errors in the eighteenth century, only in 1921 were the modern-day borders of Pennsylvania, Maryland, and Delaware officially established in this contested territory. "A scenic valley incised into the rolling Piedmont terrain of southeastern Pennsylvania and northwestern Delaware," White Clay Creek formed from magma that cooled and crystallized hundreds of millions of years ago. The Lenape, who lived in the area for some twelve thousand years before European settlers arrived, gave the creek its name, translated into Swedish and then English. Though the area was mostly farmland, the creek powered wood and flour mills in the seventeenth and early eighteenth centuries, and in the nineteenth century small entrepreneurs mined feldspar deposits for the ceramics industry and to build dams. After World War II, fears of suburbanization and encroachments by E. I. DuPont de Nemours and Company stoked preservation efforts. The White Clay Creek preserve became public land, jointly owned by Delaware and Pennsylvania, in 1984, the same year that my family and I moved from the former state to the latter.[1]

1 Rodger T. Faill, "White Clay Creek Preserve, Chester County, Pennsyl-

Growing up at the intersection of Pennsylvania, Delaware, and Maryland, I traversed what in Martha's time (and, I learned later, mine) was some of the most contested territory in the nation: the borders between two slave states and a free – or at least freer – one. I reveled then in living in Pennsylvania, in being on the right side of the Mason-Dixon Line. Recent history told a different story.

"We were a part of white flight," my mom told me once. After I was born, in 1981, my mom stopped teaching at the small Catholic school across the street. They had not planned to send me there; MacClary Elementary, the local public school, was a "good" school when my parents moved to the neighborhood in the mid-1970s, but they did not want me attending school with Black children bused in from Wilmington. Rumors of small white children supposedly being beaten up by these newcomers circulated among my parents' white friends.

My family fled across the border to Pennsylvania in 1984, when my brother was born. The new house was bigger, the new neighborhood solidly middle-class and entirely white, a product of the 1970s filled with an eclectic mix of houses, neither the identical models of 1950s Levittowns nor the bloated McMansions of the 1990s and pre-recession 2000s. My parents were a decade younger than I am now when we moved into the house, purchased and maintained for several years on a single income.

Stokely Carmichael (later Kwame Ture) and Charles V. Hamilton coined the term "institutional racism" in 1967, but the concept didn't filter down to regular white Baby Boomers like my parents until nearly fifty years later. For my own parents, it was the 2015 mistaken arrest of unimpeachably

---

vania, and New Castle County, Delaware—A Scenic Valley and the Arc Corner", *Pennsylvania Geological Survey*, 4th ser., Trail of Geology 16–020.0, 1991, 1. [Available online]

Crosshatch

respectable Black tennis player James Blake. If it could happen to him, they realized, it could happen to any Black person. As long as they didn't understand that structural racism existed, though, they couldn't condone attempts to address it – busing, perhaps, least of all.

On May 19, 1976, a panel of three federal judges in US district court ordered in a two-to-one decision the consolidation of eleven New Castle County, Delaware, school districts – Wilmington School District, which was 84.7 percent Black, DeLaWarr School District, which was 54.9 percent Black, and nine suburban school districts, which averaged at over 90 percent white – to effect desegregation. Newark School District, which I would have attended, was 94.2 percent white. The order was made possible by a March 27, 1974, ruling that the state of Delaware had intentionally worked to keep suburban school districts white, thereby contributing to segregation. Delaware was a slave state and a Jim Crow state; its largest city, Wilmington, was a place of terror to such individuals as Frederick Douglass and Harriet Tubman. But this glaring blemish on the state's history forced it to reckon with its racial legacy in a way that its neighbor Pennsylvania did not feel compelled to do. Today the former slave state is more reliably liberal than the abolitionist stronghold.

The new super-district was to be 78.5 percent white, with Black enrollment of between 10 and 35 percent in each grade. Desegregation efforts would begin in the 1977–78 school year, with schools required to show results by the following school year. Under the ruling, a five-member interim school board would determine how desegregation would be effected; though the order did not mandate busing, the examples of other localities suggested that it would be necessary to achieve the desired results. The plan would affect about eighty thousand students, with approximately fifteen thousand bused in or out of the city. It had been twenty-two years since the *Brown v. Board* decision, which found school segregation unconstitutional, and twenty since Brown II, which mandated that integration be accomplished "with all deliberate speed."

In the wake of the district court ruling, white parents protested, moved, or sought schooling alternatives. Small business owner Jim Venema had already founded an antibusing organization, the Positive Action Committee (PAC), in February 1975. By the end of that year, the organization had five thousand members, mostly middle-class, suburban whites. Within months, signs indicated a massive wave of white flight out of New Castle County and into Chester County, Pennsylvania, and Cecil County, Maryland. White families flocked, for example, to a neighborhood in Maryland where the builder promised to "let your children walk to neighborhood schools." It was an ironic reenactment of Douglass and Tubman's journey – or, more distantly and more abstractly, the Quaker migration to North America. These white parents, too, thought they were seeking freedom, though the term meant something very different to them. In the meantime, with so many homes newly on the market in Delaware, housing values declined. Those committed to remaining in Delaware increasingly turned to private or parochial schools if they could afford it, while public schools expected declining enrollments.[2]

Some Delaware parents went so far as to found their own schools to avoid busing. One of the first was in Claymont, Delaware, just ten minutes from Wilmington by car but a world away demographically; its public schools were 94.9 percent white. Claymont Community School (CCS), which intended to serve grades one through nine starting in the fall of 1977, had six hundred students enrolled within two months of the court order. School president Carl Aley minced no words:

2 Linda Loyd, "Busing: Delawareans Begin Evasion Tactics," *Philadelphia Inquirer*, July 18, 1976.

Crosshatch

"We formed to provide a reasonable alternative to busing ... We wanted to eliminate any violent reaction to hard forced busing. There's been violence in other places – Boston, Louisville – and it only occurs when citizens are up against a wall." Angry whites could not be blamed, he implied, if the government forced them to lash out this way.

In the most famous image from the Boston busing crisis, the Pulitzer Prize–winning "The Soiling of Old Glory," a white teenager attacks Black civil rights lawyer Ted Landsmark with an American flag.

Shortly after my family moved to Pennsylvania, a new neighbor summed up the situation with the local schools. "The schools here are good," she told my mom, "if only there weren't so many Mexicans." We were in close proximity to Kennett Square, a mushroom-farming hub that attracted a large number of immigrants, but my elementary school was almost all white. At any rate, it didn't work out in the longterm; the public schools weren't challenging enough for me, apparently. My mom went back to teaching in the spring of 1990, at a school my parents hoped would be a good fit for my brother and me.

In 1978, a group of parents from Newark and the Wilmington suburbs rented space in a local shopping center. Below a karate studio and above a Dunkin' Donuts, around the corner from a local grocery store and a Rite Aid, they founded a school. For the next five years, the school called this location home.

At first, the group tried to emulate what Dr. Henry S. Myers had accomplished in Pasadena, California: the establishment of a publicly funded "fundamental school." According to Myers in his book *Fundamentally Speaking*, "A fundamental school is simply a school where the basics of education are stressed with little or no experimentation: where discipline reigns and where patriotism flourishes."

This vision appealed to the Delaware parents, but local school boards were not game. Instead, the group established their own private fundamental school, with an English teacher from Newark High School as headmaster.

A devout Catholic educated at Cardinal Hayes High School and Manhattan College in the Bronx, the new headmaster had resisted society's secular drift from the early 1960s. In retrospect, he recalled later, "the early 1960s were halcyon … Music was still melodic and fairly innocent, late doo-wop and all that, and the 'end' of dating was, for most of us, matrimony … Ed Sullivan was still popular, and most respected his earlier decision not to show Elvis' rotating hips. … those innocent years ended, historians say, when JFK was killed."

No, they don't. We don't. We say that there never were any innocent years.

The upheavals of the next several years included an increased focus on student-centered education, which turned the world upside down for traditionalists like the new headmaster. His school, instead, would be like schools of the past. Its students would be like students of the past, who respected authority and God and country. The only problem was that the past he aspired to emulate — the halcyon days of midcentury — never existed. The story the new school told students about their place in history was an impossible lie.

"It's morning again in America," a 1984 campaign ad for Ronald Reagan begins. The narrator speaks in dulcet tones against the image of a receding city skyline. Like my family did that same year, the ad then quickly moves to the suburbs, showing a boy delivering newspapers and a man leaving home for work in his station wagon. The narrator emphasizes people going to work, buying homes, and getting married. Whiteness is everywhere: white suburban houses and the White House, white people getting married in white dresses.

Crosshatch

The only time the ad deviates from this uninterrupted barrage of whiteness is with a couple of kids shown staring up in awe at the American flag. Otherwise, America is equated with racial exclusivity, middle-class prosperity, and heteronormativity. Reagan, like the new headmaster, held the social revolutions of the 1960s and 1970s in his crosshairs. It'll go back to normal, he told his supporters. They've taken too much from you. You'll be back on top. Remarkably, from the perspective of forty years, his version of this message seems almost gentle.

In this context, it's not surprising that the new school reflected midcentury racial mores. From the start, officials denied that it was a white flight school, but the founding announcement came just two weeks after the local board of education established busing guidelines for the new school year, and it opened its doors on the same day that busing went into effect in northern Delaware. None of the school's original 208 students, nor any of its applicants, were Black, and no more than two were not white. Meanwhile, approximately two-thirds of the school's white students would have been bused. These statistics were so glaring that the IRS froze the school's application for tax-exempt status under proposed new regulations that would require schools founded or expanded within a year of desegregation either to enroll a certain percentage of minority students or to show that they were actively trying to recruit such students. But over the course of the next decade, the student body remained largely unchanged. Instead, suburban white kid after suburban white kid came in to take the admissions test. I was one of them.

Amid all of this yuckiness, it's difficult to admit how fundamentally my time there shaped me. I suppose it did what it was supposed to do, taking already privileged kids and cementing our status in the upper-middle class, a strategy ripped from the pages of Richard V. Reeves's *Dream Hoarders*, cushioning Millennials' oft-cited downward mobility relative to our parents. But it's also where I learned to love the mechanics of writing, the way the pieces fit together to convey meaning. It's where I learned to love history.

Because, surprisingly, my history classes — history as academic subject rather than mythology — were excellent. (Okay, most of my classes were excellent.) How strange that an institution could promulgate two such different versions of the past. But maybe the past we lived through is in nostalgia-tinged retrospect the hardest to see clearly. No wonder, in any event, that I have always felt unmoored from narrative, that I've never been able to see clearly my own place in history, which is a kind of home.

"We probably should have sent you to a Friends school," my mom later told me, after years of listening to me prattle on about feminism and her own political conversion. At the local one, in Wilmington, I could have been friends with Ashley Biden. At another time, in another Friends school, I could have been friends with Martha.

* * *

I learned something else at school, or perhaps it had been in me all along: the idea that my own life existed outside of history.

Down at the bottom of the hill outside my neighborhood, right along the creek, is an old Baptist meetinghouse. The one-room wooden structure bows little to aesthetics, though a pediment adorned the original entrance, now filled with stones. I still think about this church sometimes, the cemetery that lies behind a low, stone wall, the sexton's house across the street. I spent most of 1998 staying up late in the night to write my dystopian screenplay. I was going to film parts of it there.

At the time, the visible deterioration of the church, that

Crosshatch

irrefutable evidence that it – that *people* – had been there for a long time, jarred. It seemed far removed from my ho-hum middleclasssuburbanwhitegirllife, though it was mere yards from my house. Life felt so different from history that I couldn't imagine being so close to it.

History was people *changing the world*.

Life was all ... going to the grocery store.

How many times did Ashley, my best friend, and I walk into the woods behind our shared neighborhood looking for adventure? Late twentieth-century suburbia seemed to hold none. So we donned peasant skirts from my cache of 1970s dress-up clothes and filched bread and cheese from her mother's gleaming, well-stocked refrigerator and set off: we were princesses in disguise, on the run from evil suitors who hoped to marry us only to steal our kingdom. But once we were in the woods, what? There was no script, no plot for us to follow.

This lack of plot, this *storylessness*, gnawed at me. How much longer would I have to stay in bumblefuck, where *nothing happened, ever*? This is how I gave directions to my house for high school cast parties: Turn right at the red barn. Drive past the cornfields on your left. At least the rural back roads provided cover as my raucous theater friends and I barreled down them, singing showtunes and the top of our lungs and daring one another to take off our clothes. When last I drove through the area, I was stunned by the fulsome greenery, the way it arced over the narrow roads as if waiting to overtake them. Rural driving terrifies me now, though it was all I did growing up in southern Chester County. But I've lived in cities my entire adult life, and now it just seems *wrong* for it to get that dark.

Martha loved our provincial life, but I did not. In the grand tradition of middle-class, suburban white girls everywhere, I was very bored. I had to get out.

I wanted so much more out of life: adventure, romance,

heroism. So much more than my parents' life, than what my friends seemed to want. I wanted a *big* life, the life of an immigrant girl striker, a World War II factory worker, a Vietnam War protester. I was Dorothy, longing to escape the Kansas cornfields. Or Belle, wanting so much more than her provincial life.

(Ariel gets the best song, but she was crazy for wanting to leave the sea for the boring old land. *Bet they don't reprimand their daughters?* Hahaha. That's *all they do*.)

It was Belle whom I pictured as Ashley and I traipsed through the woods. Belle, who promised that even quiet, bookish girls could escape their stultifying small-town lives (setting aside this story's gender issues for just a moment, which is something I rarely say).

The life that I clamored for seemed to exist in two places: history and movies – well, culture generally, but movies especially. I tried both, in a manner of speaking.

I wasn't bold enough to try to *be* these women, exactly. I thought perhaps I could portray them on stage or screen, which turned out not to be true. It still required too much actual life experience. Perhaps, I thought later, resigning myself to even greater distance, I could study them. This I could do, to an extent.

I have spent my entire writing career, perhaps my entire life, trying to answer these questions: What kinds of experiences do women get to have, and what kinds of experiences do we value? What kinds of experiences do we deem worth writing about? It certainly wasn't my own.

I think I wrote this book in part to disabuse myself of this notion. If Martha's life was worth writing about, then maybe mine was too.

Like her, I have history in my blood. So do we all. But it didn't feel that way. There's nothing wrong with my family's history, two sturdy limbs of mostly decent, hardworking Cath-

Crosshatch

olics who did the very best they could, immigrants of various nineteenth- and twentieth-century waves – potato famine, Ellis Island, Eastern bloc refugees – and their descendants, people so committed to education that, though my father was the first in his family to go to college, only one generation later almost half of my Larocco cousins and I are doctors. I can even understand why my parents were Republicans until a few years ago, coming of age as they did during the Cold War, one with relatives under dictators, the other at odds with a federal government that had tried to make him fight in a war he did not believe in. Theirs is an inspiring story and a frustrating story, like so much of the history of the white middle-class.

Family history is a big deal to a lot of people, like the retirees who flock to the genealogy courses at my work. DNA tests too. I've never been interested in DNA tests because the results don't come with *stories*. Sign me up when Ancestry can guarantee that each test also comes with your great-grandmother's diary. One of mine was an Italian immigrant and union member in early twentieth-century New York City. Tell me more about *that*. Names and dates I have.

Which, I know, not everyone does.

I know there are stories in my family's history: one grandmother who survived an abusive, alcoholic father, another who was evacuated with her two children from Hungary to Austria, huddled on a Red Cross train with British bombers overhead while her husband was a prisoner of war. In the early 1980s, when my parents and I still lived in Delaware, Joe Biden helped my mom get some of her relatives out of Romania.

Why aren't these stories enough? Why, all my life, have I imagined an alternate ancestry for myself? There are my imagined Quaker ancestors, who fought against slavery in the nineteenth century and became conscientious objectors in the twentieth; and my Eastern European Jewish immigrant ancestors, who joined the International Ladies Garment Workers Union, marched in the 1909 strike, and witnessed the Triangle Shirtwaist fire two years later, mourning their lost friends.

Perhaps this is why I became a historian: to justify my grasping, vulture-like theft of everyone else's stories. To make it seem okay, a vocation rather than an appropriation.

* * *

Forays into historical memory mitigated my girlhood malaise. Philadelphia, New York City, and Washington, DC, were all within a day's drive. In those days, the Museum of American History at the Smithsonian was darker and twistier, with an ice cream shop in the basement and a huge, wood-paneled bookstore. These ancillary parts were my favorites, places where I could ingest history or bring it home with me.

More troubling was the nearby natural history museum, which I could barely walk into. I could not get past the Tyrannosaurus rex in the entranceway. As my dad and brother forged ahead, my mom and I watched a video about the origins of life on Earth, a topic I was too young to understand the incomprehensibility of.

I once confessed on a first date that I am terrified of Pangea. Supercontinents in general, really: Gondwanaland, which predated and eventually collided with Pangea. Pannotia. Ur. Valbarra. The names alone seem not of this earth. There's something about the size of these land masses, the idea of being stuck in the middle of a supercontinent without ever being able to see the ocean. Or, worse, of being lost *in* that ocean. I cannot hold all of it — the geological scale and sweep of time — in my head at once. It is too much for me to contemplate.

Crosshatch

Then there are the supercontinents that will inevitably form hundreds of millions of years in the future. How do we go on, knowing that? How do we make it matter? I contemplate all of this in a natural history museum.

American history museums, and the history they contain, feel just the right size. I can fit their content into my head, internalize it, contemplate it without existentialist dread. I can recognize it as history.

My date, for some reason, found this quirk adorable. He was sweet, but I only saw him one more time. Poor guy, he humored me on our second date by spending hours playing an insidiously complicated board game based on the 1960 election. He even let me be Kennedy.

* * *

In 2015, after I had crashed and burned in academia, I moved back to Pennsylvania from Washington, DC. I was done with it all: the despair and anxiety of adjuncting, the fruitlessness of the tenure-track job search, the loneliness. I was ready to do anything. I didn't expect to find a job that I love at a place that, hilariously, holds the papers of the family that in the eighteenth century owned the land on which my childhood home sits. Circle, consider yourself full.

Were there other reasons, beyond my professional failures, that I returned? Some possibilities:

When Ashley and I wandered too far from home on our princess adventures, I got in trouble, even if I didn't know I had transgressed a boundary, even if I didn't know that boundary existed. Once, we walked down the street to an older girl's house. She showed us how to put on makeup in her ballet shoe-strewn bedroom. It seemed so innocent, but my mom was furious at me when I got home. I didn't know why. I never did.

Soon this feeling – this voice telling me that I had done something wrong, even if I didn't know it – pervaded my life, even when doing something innocuous as catching lightning bugs with neighbors on a summer night. It's never really gone away.

Was that the voice that called me home, back to Pennsylvania, that made me think that being anywhere else was bad? That made me think that perhaps, if I went home, I would finally be *good*?

Or was it that, when something actually happened, it was *too actual*? Consider:

Mrs. Healy's semi-annual voice recitals were always at the Presbyterian church in downtown Newark, the one with the great acoustics, next to the galleria with the best coffee shop but not the one my friends and I hung out in. Our hearts belonged to Jammin' Java, somewhere between barebones and shabby but open late(ish) and with free parking.

At almost every recital, someone sang composer Marta Keen Thompson's "Homeward Bound." I never did. Most commonly it was Mrs. Healy's niece Tori, whose alto tones gave it resonance that my middling-quality soprano, wavery and small when nervous, never could. Toward the end of the program each winter and spring, my heart already raw from the little old man who sang "Danny Boy," his adorable wife in the audience, eyes gleaming, I heard Mrs. Papilli play the opening chords of "Homeward Bound" and tried not to cry. Google "Homeward Bound Mormon Tabernacle Choir." It won't disappoint.

At the last of these, in June of 2000, I was eighteen and two months away from *getting out*. In the first part of the song, the narrator yearns to escape a provincial life: "Bind me not to the pasture / Chain me not to the plow." Yes, *YES*, my heart shouted. The promise to return "when adventure's lost its meaning" never resonated with me. When would that be?

Crosshatch

When on earth would cornfields hold more appeal than sky-scrapers?

A year and change later, I trudged to my reviled and required Friday morning dance class. I'm not graceful, and I could never remember the steps, which my teacher seemed to think I did intentionally, or at least that I could have remembered them if I just tried a little harder. But my brain didn't work that way.

The only part of the class I enjoyed was when the teacher played the Eva Cassidy version of "Fields of Gold," a melancholy song made more so by the singer's early death. As in "Homeward Bound," the narrator promises a loved one to return to their shared rural roots: "I never made promises lightly / And there have been some that I've broken / But I swear in the days still left / We'll walk in fields of gold."

There was a lot to think about on this particular Friday in September 2001. Was this the moment that I decided to return home someday? I didn't think so at the time, and I hadn't thought so the day before, when I told my parents of my plan to return to the city from my roommate's house on Long Island, against their wishes and in spite of their tears. My dad had to walk away from the phone.

"It's my home now," I told them, ridiculously, as if being a college student somewhere is anything like living there. As if it's anything like being home.

Once, in grad school, I got into an argument with some folks in a different department about the concept of home-space, which as far as I can tell means, well, home.

"What do we mean by *home-space?*" the professor asked. The students nodded meditatively for a moment before one volunteered, "I think it means the place that exists outside of capitalism." More meditative nodding. I inhaled deeply.

"But that's ridiculous," I responded, "the only reason we think of home the way we do — as a refuge, as a place separate from productive labor, is *because of* capitalism." One might as well say that home exists *outside of history*.

(For decades, I realize, I said this about my own home.)

This went on for a while. I'll spare you most of it. But it pleased me greatly that the instructor wrote furiously in his notebook as I spoke.

Thavolia Glymph: "Home as a political figure and space comes into focus only when a key misconception is set aside: that the household is a private sphere."[3]

Even knowing all of this, the truth is that I never could stay away from southeastern Pennsylvania, from which I had once longed to escape.

Internet satire sites gently mock me for these feelings. *Reductress* asks, "Should You Write a Memoir or Are You Just Back Home for the Weekend?" "It can be stressful returning to your hometown as an adult," the lede notes, "Your old friends aren't around, family is a lot to handle, and of course, you have to decide whether or not your passing observations have any literary merit." *The Onion* lists "your hometown" as one of the five "best cities for millennials." Along with an "unshakable sensation that you both belong here and are a stranger here," the price of admission is only "admission of defeat."[4]

I chuckle and groan in recognition. We Millennials entered our forties in a nostalgic state of mind.

* * *

---

3 Thavolia Glymph, *Out of the House of Bondage: The Transformation of the Plantation Household* (Cambridge: Cambridge University Press, 2008), 3.

4 Gabi Shiner, "Quiz: Should You Write a Memoir or Are You Just Back Home for the Weekend?" Reductress, Dec. 11, 2019, https://reductress.com/post/should-you-write-memoir-or-home-for-weekend/; "Best Cities for Millennials," The Onion, Sept. 16, 2014, https://www.theonion.com/best-cities-for-millennials-1841771152.

Crosshatch

I haven't succumbed entirely. I live in Philadelphia, the beautiful garbage city that saved the country in the 2020 election and maybe played a role in its history before then. But twice that year I asked myself what would happen if I had to leave the city. The first time was in June, when protests and riots broke out over the murder of George Floyd. National Guard members occupied Fifty-Second Street, the main corridor of Black-owned businesses, nonchalantly eating pizza and leaning on their tanks alongside boarded-up storefronts. The second time was in October, when violence hit closer to home with the murder of Walter Wallace Jr. in the next neighborhood over from mine.

I know well Martha's cry that she had disappointed her mother. These are the feelings that emerge when I think about the fact that I've spent my adult life in ways that make my parents afraid for me – places where there are terrorist attacks and police shootings, concrete blocks instead of backyards.

There was nothing (for me) to be scared of, of course. But still, what if? Should I make sure the car had gas? Pack a bag of essentials? And what about the kitties?

Part of white privilege, of class privilege, is that I have relatives in the suburbs, members of those generations that grew up in cities, fled, and now are horrified that I ride the subway alone. My aunt in Bucks County even offered me her guest room. But those of us who have the resources to leave the city also have the least to fear from it.

One night that summer, a young woman yelled at Josh, my boyfriend, and me while we slept. It was late, and he had asked her to turn her music down. He's more likely to get involved than I am, more inclined to leave notes for his neighbors about their untidy garbage or to tut-tut the gentlemen who gather outside the liquor store / fake Chinese food restaurant at the end of the block. They're mostly guys who grew up on the block but had to move when they got priced out. Across the street, they've erected a memorial of liquor bottles to a young man who recently died. This young woman was friends with him.

"Nobody wants you here, white boy!" she yelled from the street, over and over again. "Fuck you, and fuck your white bitch girlfriend!" This part I actually found hilarious. That's me!

She was right, of course, to be angry at gentrification, at the ways her neighborhood continues to change. White people moving into long-abandoned, identically rehabbed houses. Condos going up at the end of the block. Another neighbor, also white, opened his window and threatened to call the police.

I knew that Josh just wanted to sleep, to feel at home in the house that he spent a decade saving for. I knew he chose this location to be close to the pottery studio where he throws the beautiful bowls and plates and mugs that line his cupboards. I, on the other hand, have always been a little too excited about all of the coffee shops within walking distance, places that I could bring my laptop and sit and write and look moody and artistic and think deep, creative thoughts.

Complicity, *c'est moi*. Philadelphia, like most cities, makes it impossible to forget this. Rightfully so.

Perhaps this is part of why others of my generational cohort left cities in droves for suburban and rural areas in 2020, leaving their cool, urban lives, those middle fingers to our Baby Boomer parents, for quieter environs more akin to those in which we were raised. These were the places people romanticized, far away from high infection rates and long lines at the grocery store, from mysterious nightly fireworks and National Guard members on street corners. "Please stop writing 'Why I Left New York' Pandemic Essays," begged *Huffpost* writer Claire Fallon just a month into lockdown, noting that "feeling guilty about fleeing the city for greener pastures is not a sufficient reason to write a personal essay."[5]

Is this just a form of white flight? It's driven, I think, by nostalgia rather than overt racism, though in certain ways nostalgia is no less vicious a motivator. As privileged white people who have the option to do so, we want to return to our childhoods, to our homes, to a time we felt less culpable, to a time when we could comfortably imagine ourselves outside of history, to a time when people wouldn't yell at us from the street and make us confront our complicity, to a time when we could imagine ourselves not as guilty, but as, finally, good.

---

5 Claire Fallon, "Please Stop Writing 'Why I Left New York' Pandemic Essays," HuffPost, Apr. 22, 2020, https://www.huffpost.com/entry/stop-writing-why-i-left-new-york-pandemic-essays_n_5e9fa07bc5b6b2e5b839dcd3.

CHAPTER THREE: WRITER

Martha didn't get to continue her formal education beyond Sharon, though she would dearly have loved to. "I often think now that I would love to go to school for 2 or 3 years," she wrote, "do nothing but study study – yet I know such a course would ruin my health." By eighteen she was on the other side of the classroom, first at a different aunt and uncle's school in Bayside, Long Island, where she flirted with a dark-haired young man with an unflattering mustache, then in Harrison, New York, and eventually back in Philadelphia. Combined with housework, long hours both inside and outside of the classroom left little time for her own intellectual pursuits.[1]

John Bunting, Martha's first love, led a similar early life. Born the same year as Martha to a family of Darby Quakers, John's formal education ended in 1854 – sooner than he too would have liked, sooner even than Martha's. But "in 1855 he had the good fortune to form the friendship of a very beautiful and brilliant girl several years his senior and who was already engaged to be married when he first met her. During these three years she was a great stimulus to him in his literary studies." She wrote letters to him almost every day on literary subjects, and he sent his own writing to her for critique, "she

---

1 MS to SB, Mar. 11, 1860.

Fig. 7: John Bunting, n.d., in *In Memoriam*, p. 32, ed. Anna Webster Bunting et al. (Philadelphia: Friends' Book Association of Philadelphia, n.d. [1906?]), box 8, folder 1901–1904: John Bunting, Schofield Papers.

Crosshatch

herself being a writer of marked ability."[2]

I don't know any details about this woman: her name, what her relationship with John was like, what happened to her later. I don't know what she wrote, or whether and how it reflected her inner life. She exists in the historical record in only this one mention and, I suppose, buried is somewhere in John's voluminous writing, as a secret and hidden influence. But we cannot extricate her from there, we cannot extricate her from him. She does not have a voice of her own.

Who gets to speak in this world? To whom do we listen? It is not often women.

In John's memoir of childhood, written two years before his death and specifically to be published on that occasion, the epigraph borrows another woman's voice. It's Ophelia, from *Hamlet*: "There's rosemary – that's for remembrance." The words sound nice, decontextualized from the ways the men in her life drove her mad.

Neighbors and acquaintances since adolescence, John and Martha saw each other in Quaker meeting every week but did not become close until July 4, 1861. "On that day," she later wrote, "we first learned to <u>know</u> each other."[3] With her parents and sisters away, Martha found herself home alone for several days. She saw John at the post office that morning, and later he came to the house to keep her company. It was a strange Independence Day, the first of the war, one better suited to quiet contemplation than raucous celebration. John played the violin for Martha, and in the evening the two sat outside and watched the fireworks slice through the calm, still air. A comet arced through the sky. Known as the Thatcher or War Comet, the phenomenon was visible in the North in late spring and summer 1861. It hadn't been seen since the fifteenth century; it won't be back until the twenty-third. We

2 Anna W. Bunting, "After Years," in Bunting, *In Memoriam*, 32.
3 MS to SB, July 15, 1863.

missed it. John and Martha reached an understanding about their relationship that night, the date of which Martha commemorated for years to come. It was the sweetest friendship she had ever known.

* * *

Two weeks later, *Scientific American* explained to its readers the trajectories of parabolic comets, which come close to Earth only once before drifting forever farther away. The Thatcher Comet had piqued reader interest in bolides of all sorts. "Light, ethereal volumes of vapor, they come from unmeasured distances above, below, or on either hand, with constantly accelerating velocity, rush in a strange turmoil around the sun, and then move more and more slowly away on their solitary courses into the depths of space."[4]

Would John and Martha's relationship be like a parabolic comet? She hoped not − not like a comet, not like anything else that lit up the sky before disintegrating. Their friendship could not,

> must not be, like the fiery rockets
> That rose in beauty − burst & fell − nor
> The blazing meteor that shone with
> Dazzling brightness, & went out in gloom.
> But as the quiet star shining on forever,
> Always there, tho' shadows intervened and
> Brighter light, obscures the constant ray.[5]

After July 4, John and Martha wrote to each other almost daily, long letters full of feeling. They took trips together, once to Castle Rock in New York, and went on walks and outings.

4 "The Mystery of Comets' Tails," *Scientific American*, July 20, 1861.
5 MS to JB, July 4, 1863.

Crosshatch

In August they went to Rye, New York, where they "took a sweet walk down to the <u>brook</u> and then over in the woods where we rested under 'our double tree.'" They were fond of Tennyson and sometimes brought his work with them on walks; perhaps they read to each other. On a ferry ride in September, they "sat watching the waves, beneath which were reflected the bright stars, till near midnight," then rose early to watch the sun rise over the ocean. They attended concerts and lectures and together ran a Lyceum, a place for young people to debate political and philosophical issues. The group also produced a paper, for which John wrote regularly. Martha called him "the poet."[6]

Write a piece, she asked him one night as they sat outside. He came to the house often now, at times when Martha was alone. That night the stars were dim, and every now and then clouds obscured the moon.[7]

He obliged with a piece full of "deep beauty." But Martha did not trust her own reading, and so she sent the poem to Sadie Brouwer, her best friend, for confirmation. Sadie, too, found John's poems beautiful, though she asked Martha to explain the parts she "did not exactly understand." Neither woman felt qualified to judge the work on her own. "My poor pen could not do it half justice," Martha wrote of another poem John shared with her.[8]

In 1862, John included in a letter a response to Martha's desire for a "better life." He gave her some good advice, including the need to empathize with others:

> Learn first the agony of other souls,
> And as the great years' wheel majestic rolls

---

6 MS diary, Aug. 30, 31, 1861, Sept. 3, 4, 1862.
7 MS to SB, Sept. 17, 1861.
8 MS to SB, Sept. 17, 1861; SB to MS, Sept. 22, 1862; MS diary, Nov. 17, 1861.

> Mark how the heart strings of the people smart ...
> Thy better life must act as well as feel;
> From thy heart's stony-barred depths must steal
> To thy poor brother, sympathy's sweet balm.[9]

Empathy and simplicity, confidence in one's choices even or especially if they contradicted mainstream society, are fine values, well in line with reformist tendencies among nineteenth-century Friends, and qualities Martha already strove to cultivate. But ultimately, and precisely for these reasons, I find John's advice irritating. For him, internal changes were enough. "A better life!" he began the poem, "O first a better heart! / Weed out the gall, the passion and pride; / The fetters grasp with which thy soul is tied."[10]

What was a woman like Martha to do with this advice? Purifying her heart and soul would not produce the "better life" she sought. She would still be bound by the same constraints of nineteenth-century middle-class womanhood, which largely restricted her to marriage or teaching. John could not have understood this dilemma, which left in Martha's heart "a longing, a great thirsting after something it feels it needs." Her material comforts, her family's love could "not satisfy the souls needs."[11]

Perhaps I'm not being entirely fair to John here: John, who hoped to become a writer or musician but found himself caught up in the gears of nineteenth-century capitalism, who saw his dreams stamped out by the exigencies of time and money.

Martha did not share my frustration with this poem. She thought it was just lovely. "How can I be sufficiently thankful," she wrote the day she received it, "for such blessings which

---

9 John Bunting, "A Better Life," in Bunting, *In Memoriam*, 43.

10 Bunting, "A Better Life," 43.

11 MS diary, Dec. 1, 1861, Feb. 21, 1862.

will live with me always guiding and helping me onward to that 'Better life' which I so long for, Heaven help me attain it, by cleansing my soul of all imperfections, and obeying the truths which will be shown me if faithful to God." Decades later, the poem was included in John's memorial. Martha penciled in a scribbled confession that she was already planning to seek her better life elsewhere.

"Homeward Bound": Bind me not to the pasture / Chain me not to the plow.

Belle: I want so much more than this provincial life.

* * *

Martha rarely wrote her own poetry, and when she did she thought it worthless. She wrote a poem for John in 1863, then immediately regretted it. She sent a copy to Sadie:

> If thee wont critizise <u>too</u> <u>much</u> or think I am vain I will send thee a little piece I wrote to him on 4th of July, <u>no one</u> else has seen it, I dont like to be made fun of. I was sweeping my room and wrote line at a time without stopping my work − . Sent it to him that day & was <u>real</u> <u>sorry</u> afterwards because I thought it was not poetry at all and he might <u>think</u> I was trying to do what I could not − . I never <u>try</u> to write it because I am <u>no</u> <u>genius</u> and do not like to aim at what I am <u>not</u> <u>capable</u> of <u>doing</u>. This was no effort − and is not worth much.[12]

This was how women had to write − how they often still have to write − one line at a time in between domestic tasks and apologies, the rhythm of their work, the demands on their time, the gendered limitations of their lives inscribed in the very act of writing. It's the invisible truth that exists between

12 MS to SB, July 15, 1863.

each line of poetry, the form itself dependent on the particular version of patriarchy that middle-class white women experienced in the mid-nineteenth century industrialized North. Even mitigated by Quakerism, it was a culture that placed little value on women's experiences.

The finding aid calls Martha's piece a "Poem about Gettysburg" because of the date, and it is, to some extent: "The crushing tread of War has left / Its footprints on the <u>Nation's heart</u>." But it's primarily about the anniversary of her friendship with John. It asks,

> How has it been with us? Thee and thy friend
> That just two years ago – stood beneath the
> Summer night, till some <u>silent power</u>
> Awoke the <u>deeper feelings</u> – dropped the seed
> Of faith & trust, formed the slender chord
> That since has grown in strength & linked
> Two hearts with friendships sacred tie – .[13]

Two copies of the poem dot a box otherwise full of correspondence, filed between two letters from Martha to Sadie. A small envelope, soft with age, is bundled with them. Marked "personal," it includes a line drawn down the middle. On one side are "John" and "past"; on the other is "present." Martha, of course, had no one to recopy these poems for her. Any copy she wanted – the one she wrote while sweeping, the one she sent to John, and the one she sent to Sadie – she had written out herself.

* * *

It's a bit of a cruel joke that John once described himself as Martha's amanuensis, the person responsible for committing

---

13 MS, "July 4th, 1863."

Crosshatch

her thoughts to paper. "Amanuensis" derives from the Latin phrase *servus a manu*, meaning "slave with secretarial duties." Manu, literally hand, also gave us manuscript. Various linguistic traditions have used it to describe both the person and the process, one who transcribes and the transcription itself, though the former is more common in modern English. While in certain cases it has been transmuted into titles for government officials and other high-status roles, it most commonly retains its association with low status and today is used synonymously with secretary: one who takes dictation or types handwritten notes, roles that became feminized over the course of the late nineteenth and twentieth centuries as the upwardly mobile office clerk — which John was — gave way to the secretarial pool. John had more time than Martha, who sometimes dictated to him while doing chores around the house.

But John, not Martha, was supposed to be the writer, and a good writer does not necessarily a good amanuensis make. They are opposite processes, after all: one depends on the assertion of the self, the other on its burial. It's a form of literary coverture, one public face to the creative soul. I think of John's friend from early adulthood, who has disappeared from the historical record entirely, whose thoughts and insights we know only thirdhand, based on how they affected John. No wonder Martha didn't want to marry, even if Pennsylvania had recently started allowing married women to own property. Property ownership didn't guarantee literary ownership.

Now I am Martha's amanuensis, her secretary, or, perhaps, her midwife. For most of the time I was writing this book, I took pictures of her letters and diary entries on my phone in the archive, uploading them to Google photos when I got home. There, on my large monitor, I could zoom in on her nineteenth-century script, adjust the saturation and contrast to make her pencil strokes easier to read. Even then, I'm lucky that her writing is (relatively) easy to read. Try deciphering fellow abolitionist and feminist Lucretia Mott's handwriting sometime. Occasionally one of my cats deleted an image or two when she walked across my keyboard, but it was okay; I just retook the picture the next time I was in the archive.

In the past several years, archivists have digitized many of Martha's papers, which is wonderful. But there's still something to be said for holding the actual documents in your hand. Secrets lurk in the rough edges of a torn-out diary page, imperceptible in two dimensions. The screen makes it difficult to perceive what *isn't* there.

I took notes on her writing on my computer, sometimes summarizing her thoughts but more often transcribing long passages and even whole documents. "It may surprise the uninitiated to learn that the hours spent in the library consulting the documents are often hours spent recopying them word for word," Arlette Farge reveals:

> The allure of the archives passes through this slow and unrewarding artisanal task of recopying texts, section after section, without changing the format, the grammar, or even the punctuation. Without giving it too much thought. Thinking about it constantly. As if the hand, through this task, could make it possible for the mind to be simultaneously an accomplice and a stranger to this past time and to these men and women describing their experiences. As if the hand, by reproducing the written syllables, archaic words, and syntax of a century long past, could insert itself into that time more boldly than thoughtful notes ever could.[14]

By being an amanuensis, I often find myself stymied when

14 Arlette Farge, *The Allure of the Archives* (New Haven, CT: Yale University Press, 2013), 15, 17.

Crosshatch

research turns to writing, unable to see the forest for the trees, producing shitty first drafts that read more like trial transcripts than literary works. "Martha wrote this ... then the next day she wrote this" and so on. But I like this arrangement: the reversal of power involved in me, a twenty-first century woman, copying down Martha's words. Eventually I figure out how to give them shape. I can do this, in part, because I have no sweeping to do. I have all of the time in the world to give to her, time she did not have herself.

CHAPTER FOUR: ARCHIVIST

It's tempting with all of this research, all of these hours spent recopying her words, to think that I know everything about Martha. But for all of the time I spent with her, I still do not know how she truly felt about John. In diaries she called him *mon ami, mein Lieber,* (rarely) "my darling." Perhaps putting it in English — putting it baldly and transparently — made it too real, too easily spotted by the nosy historian. In letters she called him "my friend." They were like brother and sister, she insisted to others. "It is not love to end in marriage," she wrote. "Dearly as I have & do love him, I have <u>never wished</u> that he might be <u>nearer</u> than a friend. In my very first letter to him, I forbid any other, & he has been nice & faithful to me."[1]

I never know whether to believe her professions of platonic love. Others in her life, including her mother, certainly had trouble doing so. "People may think we have no right to be this intimate," she wrote, "but we have." She refused to heed her mother's calls to end the relationship.[2]

Katherine Smedley, the only person to write a full-length biography about Martha, didn't take her at her word. "Like many Victorian women," Smedley wrote, Martha "resented their [sexual feelings'] power to disturb an otherwise ordered

1 MS diary, Nov. 19, 1861; MS to SB, July 15, 1863.
2 MS diary, Apr. 8, 1862.

and peaceful life ... she waged a desperate — but not always successful — battle to deny them and persuade herself that every relationship with a member of the opposite sex was one of pure friendship." Perhaps, but I find myself irritated by this insistence on not believing her. Why do we think that we understand how Martha felt better than she herself did? The skepticism her mother and others voiced annoyed Martha, too.[3]

But this is how historians learn how to do history. We are trained not to take people at their word, to probe their writing for deeper meaning, to prove that they meant the opposite of what they said. This is especially true of those precious instances when historical figures reveal their personal lives to us, and especially *especially* true of when it is women telling us whom they loved.

Journals are etchings, not existence, breadcrumbs leaving a trail to a house you will never reach. I will never find Martha, not really. But, to write her biography, I have to believe that I will.

I have to try, for example, to determine what happened between John, Martha, and a young woman named Anna Webster, a nineteen-year-old fellow teacher from Massachusetts, in the fall of 1861. Anna was frail and delicate, and surely lonely. She and her younger sister had moved to Darby with their parents, but only the two daughters remained. Martha quickly took Anna under her wing.

She was not the only one who took an interest in the newcomer. John did, too.

It was not a happy time for Martha. The days grew shorter and colder. The war continued. John and Anna fell in love.

On the last night of the year, Anna and Martha spent several hours talking in Martha's classroom. The conversa-

---

3 Smedley, *Martha Schofield and the Re-Education of the South, 1839–1916*, 38.

tion broke Martha's heart as never before. Was this when she found out about John and Anna's relationship?

It could have been something else entirely. Martha also feared for her brother, to whom she "wrote a long ernest letter" after talking to Anna. Did Anna tease Martha about the possibility of her brother having to serve in the military? Remark on the possible repercussions of his ever-growing debts?[4]

I thought perhaps that Anna found John and Martha's friendship strange, but she doesn't seem to have cared, which of course is worse. "I want thee ... not to distrust me, as thee constantly does by asking me if I am offended because thee occasionally writes notes to him &c. &c.," Anna later wrote. Why would she be offended by someone who clearly posed no threat? Anna was blunt.[5]

Martha once warned Sadie that she would probably not like Anna at first. "I do not believe thee would be much struck with her at first," she admitted, "but thee would feel kindly toward her for my sake and perhaps after awhile thee would learn to love her." Martha was Anna's only close female friend.[6]

Perhaps Martha thought John himself no longer wished to be close to her now that he had Anna. John was tired of her, she now realized. How had she not seen it before — "that some love well, but get tired, & turn to new friends forgetting the old ones"?[7]

I may be imagining this all wrong. Perhaps there was no love triangle, platonic or otherwise, after all. Perhaps the love triangle is just the easiest narrative to impose. It says more about me than it does about Martha, John, and Anna that

---

4 MS diary, Dec. 31, 1861.
5 Anna Webster to MS, n.d. [July 1863].
6 MS to SB, May 1, 1864.
7 MS diary, Feb. 21, 1862.

I can't think of any other way to make sense out of their relationship. What happened to taking her at her word, to believing what she tells me about her feelings?

I am influenced, perhaps, by *Little Women*, with Martha as Jo, John as Laurie, and Anna as Amy (though Martha identified with Beth. Who identifies with Beth?). Even there, though, I must remember that Jo refused Laurie's proposal because she simply didn't love him the way he loved her. She simply didn't want to be more than friends.

In any event, Amy's other betrayal — burning Jo's manuscript — was far worse than marrying the boy who first loved her sister. That means that no historian will ever get to read it.

Goddamn Amy.

Martha, John, and Anna eventually found a new equilibrium. John and Martha spoke quietly in her classroom after school one day as the weak March light faded outside. One night in July, Martha and Anna talked until two in the morning. Martha would not let the conversation end until she had convinced Anna of what she had to convince everyone: she and John would never be anything closer than friends, and that was how she wanted it.

Martha tried hard to be Anna's friend. She brought her on excursions, went to church with her, and cared for her when she was sick. When Anna and her sister came down with scarlet fever, Martha gave up her own bed for them. Where once Martha and John went to concerts, lectures, and the Lyceum, now the three of them went together.

It was fine. It was all fine. Or it wasn't. I'll never know.

In the meantime, Martha developed other friendships. One was with Edward P. Wilson, whom she had known since childhood. She wanted to reform him; he wanted her to be his "true sister." As a compromise, they became friends.[8]

"I shall look for a home in thy friendship," he wrote, "give

8 Edward P. Wilson to MS, Apr. 27, 1863.

Crosshatch

me sympathy & hope & call me thy friend."[9]

First deployed in the Third Pennsylvania Cavalry, by 1863 Edward was a lieutenant serving as Brigadier General Isaac J. Wistar's aide-de-camp. He and Martha wrote often during his deployment. Martha knew how it looked.

"Of course if people discover our frequent correspondence, our names will be connected," she told Sadie. "I shall be <u>sorry</u>, but will be true to him, thee, my darling, may know that he & I can <u>never be nearer than friends. Remember this.</u> He understands it & we are satisfied – ."[10]

Others did not understand. Home on business in the spring of 1863, Edward donned his Union blues and visited Martha frequently. Neighbors were suspicious.

"It need not hurt us," Martha insisted. She knew what she was doing. She would not let herself be hurt.[11]

Yet I think she was – hurt, that is. At some point she cut a word, possibly a name, out of one of Edward's letters, something she often did when sad or ashamed. Why did this keep happening to her?

* * *

When I tell friends and colleagues this story, they comment on its cinematic nature. Will Martha and John end up together? Is their story *The Way We Were* or *When Harry Met Sally*? Can men and women even *be* friends?

Of course they can. It's not 1989. Or 1862.

Even in the nineteenth century, some idealistic souls believed such friendships were possible. Agatha Lee, the protagonist of Clara Jessup (Mrs. Bloomfield H.) Moore's 1876 novel *On Dangerous Ground; or, Agatha's Friendship. A Romance of*

---

9 Wilson to MS, Apr. 27, 1863.

10 MS to SB, June 8, 1863.

11 MS to SB, June 8, 1863.

American Society, was one of them. "It had been the desire of Agatha's life," Moore wrote, "to have a Platonic friendship" – a union of souls unencumbered by sex. It's not difficult to guess how this desire works out for Agatha; the novel's entire plot is laid out in the title, though it doesn't make it entirely clear what kind of book it is. I've read enough to know that there are only two options: Agatha will either die or fall madly in love. Neither outcome provides much evidence for the viability of platonic love.[12]

Martha wouldn't have approved of Agatha's life – the lavish parties, the flirting – or of reading about it: novels were an occasional indulgence at most, corrosive to the brain and the soul if not tempered with more salubrious fare. But the two women shared some commonalities. Agatha's description of her ideal friendship sounds just like Martha's characterization of her friendship with John.

When Agatha meets Carroll Tracey, the husband of her schoolmate and best friend, Millie, she at first believes she has found in him the friend she has been looking for, "one ... who I need never fear will turn into a lover."[13]

Agatha gets her comeuppance when she falls in love with Carroll. Her belief in platonic love is shattered, and she decides to remain a spinster as penance for loving a married man. Only after Millie's death are Agatha and Carroll free to be together, and the novel ends with an explicit rejection of platonic love. "Agatha's dream of Platonic love had ended for ever," Moore wrote. "She had found the friend she had longed for ...; and in finding him she had learned that no one can sustain such ideal relations as she had dreamed of sustaining, outside of married life."[14]

12 Clara Jessup (Mrs. Bloomfield H.) Moore, *On Dangerous Ground; or, Agatha's Friendship. A Romance of American Society* (Philadelphia: Porter and Coates, 1876), 3.

13 Moore, *On Dangerous Ground*, 84.

14 Moore, *On Dangerous Ground*, 339.

In real life, Martha and Moore may have crossed paths. A writer, eccentric, and philanthropist, Clara Jessup (1824–1899) married Philadelphia businessman Bloomfield H. Moore (1819–1878), a Quaker, in 1842. During the Civil War, she established the Woman's Pennsylvania Branch of the United States Sanitary Commission. Martha found the Sanitary Commission, the thrall in which its Great Central Fair held the city, tremendously irritating, though as a good Unionist she went along with it. After her husband's death, Clara Jessup Moore legally changed her name to Clara Bloomfield-Moore: she wanted more of him, a more complete, more perfect union, and his last name alone wasn't enough.

So much for platonic love.

* * *

In *The Friendships of Women* (1867), William Rounseville Alger painted a cheerier picture of relationships between men and women, though the book begins with a depressing prospect: as more women remained single, they needed friendships to provide the emotional fulfillment that romantic love otherwise would have. "Will not the large number [of women] who are denied the satisfactions of impassioned love," he wondered, "be grateful for a book which shows them what rich and noble resources they may find in this widely different, though closely kindred, sentiment?" Friendship – including friendship with men – provided an unmarried woman with a way to be happy, "in spite of this relative mutilation of her lot." (Yikes.)[15]

In these friendships (according to Alger), women provided "a holy and powerful restraint from illicit habits." They could

---

15 William Rounseville Alger, *The Friendships of Women* (1867; repr., Boston: Roberts Brothers, 1879), 2.

inspire men's better natures, as Martha hoped to do with Edward. This was what platonic love was, after all: a union of minds and souls, not bodies.[16]

I think it's entirely possible that women in this era who were told that they did not or should not desire, that their own sexual restraint was a necessary curb on men's urges – middle-class white women like Martha – internalized this belief, even at the level of their bodies. More credence to Martha's insistence that she wanted nothing from these men but friendship. Perhaps she was asexual; perhaps she just wasn't attracted to men. Or to these particular men.

Yet I find inadequate the limited terms we have available to describe these relationships: friend or lover. Ultimately, Martha's relationship with John admits the possibility of more kinds of relationships than nineteenth – or twenty-first – century discourses generally acknowledge. If it was a friendship, it was one "deeper far deeper than is generally meant that term." "I always feel safe when he is about," she wrote, "and I know he will take good care of me always." Until we invent new terms, the relationship lives in uncategorizable ambiguity.[17]

* * *

It frustrates me, of course, that the archive doesn't tell me exactly what happened between Martha, John, and Anna, or how Martha really felt about Edward. The limits of the historical record frustrated Martha, too. Often she did not know what happened to old friends, where they lived and what they were doing. Within minutes, I can find a picture of the house where my high school crush now lives.

Martha tried to preserve her memories, her archive, as best she could. She spent an evening in May 1862 rereading

16 Alger, *The Friendships of Women*, 118.
17 MS diary, Aug. 10, 1862, Dec. 31, 1864.

and organizing some 344 letters she had received over the years, "some written a long time ago, by those I have not seen for years and who are far away, some amused, others made me feel sad." In one, an acquaintance, barely a friend, wrote of her love for a dying young man. "Now," Martha wrote, "[I] have no idea where she is, only that she went two or more years ago to Montgomery Alabama, and within a year was married to a Southern gentleman – . I never even knew what became of her first love – ."[18]

She also burned some letters, though, "thinking it due to the authors of them – ." I don't understand this desire to destroy evidence, to consign to the unknown what could be known. I don't understand it from Martha in particular, though I suppose she had other priorities that outweighed her desire to preserve the record or her concern for future historians. Who hasn't done something similar?[19]

In Lin-Manuel Miranda's *Hamilton*, Eliza destroys letters from her husband, Alexander, after learning of his affair with Maria Reynolds; the real Elizabeth Schuyler Hamilton may have done so as well. Miranda gives his characters the awareness of future historians. Eliza sings: "Let future historians wonder how Eliza / Reacted when you broke her heart." But does anyone think that way except for those future historians?

It's tempting to argue that the letters and diaries that remain in Martha's papers represent a greater truth, a clearer window into Martha's heart than do the speeches and policy papers of public figures, that the direct, physical connection between her body and her pen means these documents represent her unfiltered (or less filtered) thoughts. Perhaps this is obvious; perhaps my doubt derives only from overzealous academic skepticism. All of that training in postmodernism and performance theory.

18 MS to SB, May 18, 1862.
19 MS to SB, May 18, 1862.

By the summer of 1863, John and Anna were engaged. Anna returned to Massachusetts, where she stayed for two years. She was in no hurry to return: marriage terrified her. "I do hope it will not seem so terrible to me, when I come to be John's wife, but I dread it so much," she confessed to Martha. Why did other women not seem to mind getting married? Why did she? Anna and John kept the engagement secret despite persistent rumors, and she delayed the wedding several times.[20]

Sometimes the farther away people were from each other, the more easily the historical record connects them. Martha and Anna wrote to each other more after Anna moved back to Massachusetts, the interactions that would have been conducted in person, never to be recovered, now conducted on paper. The archive is a record of absence in this way. The intimate and the everyday often lie beyond it. "People don't often write letters to people they live with," writes historian Jill Lepore.[21]

Less circumspect individuals may have discussed such intimacies in diaries, but Martha did not, not in any direct way, at least. Letters can be better for historians than diaries; the writer usually has to provide at least some context to the addressee, indirectly providing it to the historian as well. The eavesdropper, the interloper, becomes the absent interlocutor. Historians are grateful for distance sometimes.

At some point, in some form, Martha shared with Anna the story of a doomed love affair of her own. In retrospect Martha blamed its dissolution on her own pride and haughtiness. I only know this from one of Anna's letters, a mirror

---

20 Anna Webster to MS, June 2, 1865.
21 Jill Lepore, *The Secret History of Wonder Woman* (New York: Vintage Books, 2014), 309.

Crosshatch

reflecting Martha's life back to her and, through the archive, to me.

With almost all of his own letters gone, John exists as nothing so much as a lacuna at the center of Martha's correspondence with Anna and Sadie. They might not have told me that much, anyway. He never talked to Anna about Martha or vice versa.

"I would hardly know that he was acquainted with such a person as my dear Mart, from his letters," wrote Anna. Burn.[22]

I saw him only through their eyes, not because the mid-nineteenth century afforded them the power to define the men in their lives, but because the archive offers *only* this possibility. Another reversal of power. I can only ever know John through the women in his life.

The archive is a record of absence in one other way: the intimate is much more likely than is the quotidian to be destroyed by its authors.

In September 1865, shortly before she left Darby for her new teaching post, Martha returned to John the letters he had written her, and she asked him to return hers – over 400 pages' worth. She dropped many of them into the cold Atlantic the next month, en route to South Carolina. The following July, as she returned home, she disposed of another batch, some written as early as 1861 and perhaps documenting her early friendship with John. Late at night, while the rest of the passengers painted the proverbial town red, she

> went alone to the low of the Steamer, there in the stillness of the midnight, with the moon just rising, and the stars keeping guard over the waves, I kissed the dear familiar words and one by one dropped the love messages into the broad deep – . The white waves caught

22 Webster to MS, June 2, 1865.

them up, the bright sparks of phosphorous were as torches at the grave, then all was gone, gone – down down into that myriad sea, where no human eye can ever brighten at their coming.[23]

Anna and John finally married in January 1866. Anna had hoped that Martha would be there. "Thee knows thee is pledged not to get married," Anna reminded Martha, "but spend most of thy time, and have a home with me, when I am married." But Martha could not travel to Massachusetts for the wedding, and she never lived in Darby again.[24]

The wedding didn't seem to bother Martha much. "This has been a most lovely day," she wrote, "and all the time my thoughts were with my two friends at Hyde Park, for this is the day fixed for their marriage." She hoped they would be happy.[25]

Perhaps that was enough. She had a new life she had long dreamed of pursuing, and she wished her friends happiness. She was fine.

Or perhaps not. "I could fill five pages with my feelings today," she confessed to her diary, "but it is not worth-while." She took those thoughts to the grave.[26]

Before Martha returned John's letters to him, before she asked that he return her own, she kept his missives in a double locked box. No one, not even Sadie, would know how John and Martha felt about each other.

Martha's many letters are in an unlocked box now – several boxes, actually, that anyone who cares to can open. There is much to learn. But there is also much that cannot be learned.

---

23 MS diary, July 3, 1866.
24 Anna Webster to MS, Nov. 16, 1865.
25 MS diary, Jan. 18, 1866.
26 MS diary, Jan. 18, 1866.

INTERLUDE: UNFINDING AID

A decade ago, I gave a series of talks at local branches of the American Association of University Women (AAUW), which had given me money to finish my dissertation. Like many civic organizations, it's an aging organization, the median age of my audiences hovering around seventy. I was barely thirty. As I discussed the ways in which women's experiences have been delegitimized, even by radical men, heads nodded.

I talked about writer Anne Roiphe, who in the late 1950s worked as a receptionist to support her husband's writing career. When she finished typing a play of his in 1959, she felt like a muse, like "the most fortunate woman in the world." The real-life version of a muse is a secretary. The following year, at nine months pregnant, Roiphe trudged through a snowy Manhattan evening to pick her husband's typewriter up at the repair shop. On her way home, her water broke. She struggled to the nearest pay phone to call her husband, who was sleeping and would not answer the phone.

After these talks, as I made awkward small talk and helped myself to mediocre lunch buffets in freezing Hyatt or Westin conference rooms, the women in attendance told me their stories. "I typed my ex-husband's dissertation for him!" they confided over and over again. (It was always the ex.) The subtext was clear: *I could have been you if I were younger. I could have*

77

been the writer. But instead, I was the secretary, the amanuensis. John Steinbeck's wife typed *The Grapes of Wrath.*

My life must have seemed unimaginably free to these women, as in many ways it has been. I'm sure it would seem that way to Martha, too.

Of course, women's voices are still not taken as seriously as men's. At one end of the spectrum, women are silenced through the threat of violence. At the other – the best we can hope for – lies mere condescension.

* * *

In the opening scene of Lily King's *Writers and Lovers,* the protagonist, Casey, unwillingly updates her landlord on her novel. "You know," he responds, "I just find it extraordinary that you think you have something to say." The conversation was based nearly verbatim on an exchange King had as a young writer.[1]

I think here of the professor who made me cry. It was 2012, the same year I spent speaking to AAUW groups. Not all of his advice was terrible: he encouraged me to handwrite, rather than type, my dissertation. As it happened, my dissertation was already finished at the time, but he had spent the last hour and a half talking at me and so would have had no reason to know that. He didn't agree with my argument about Students for a Democratic Society (SDS), another group that loved to sideline its women members, a group to which he had belonged. It didn't matter how much evidence I had to back up my assertions; it wasn't the way he remembered it, and that was that. (Yet he liked to say that a historian is someone who tells people their memories are wrong ....) It was all very "look here, little girl." This professor was and is of the generation that had wives to type for them.

1 Lily King, *Writers & Lovers* (New York: Grove Press, 2020), ebook.

Crosshatch

I actually did not grow up composing on the computer. All through college I wrote by hand and transcribed later. I've gone back to this process lately, free writing by hand early in the morning and turning to the computer only later. Much popular psychology, backed by some research, tells us that handwriting is better, that it lights up different or maybe more parts of the brain. For me it was in the hopes of salvaging my Internet-ravaged attention span and providing some respite for my eyes, which grow tired from staring at the computer screen. Then there is the way handwriting protects me, rendering my thoughts illegible to anyone else. Letting me reveal and hide at the same time. Then, finally, there is my carpal tunnel syndrome, which continues to scream at me though I've adjusted my wrist position. But I never really learned how to type, so my finger positioning is wonky, and I rely on my right hand too much. Someday I will have to get surgery, and who will type for me while I recover?

What were these men even *doing* while their wives typed their dissertations? Sleeping, I guess, like Anne Roiphe's husband. I hope these women inserted themselves where they could, making changes without their husbands' knowledge, either to exert their own creativity or out of spite. I hope they hit the typewriter keys as loudly as possible to wake their sleeping spouses, turning secretarial work into a feminist revenge story.

* * *

I see myself in Martha's insecurities about her writing, her fears that she had overstepped her place or her abilities. Her anticipation of ridicule, her need to explain that she had barely tried, anyway. I think many women feel this way. I certainly have. I think back to all of the times I've been embarrassed by my writing, all of those earnest, unfiltered thoughts I bled onto the page and then held it up to my peers, my hand still dripping red as if from a Klingon bonding ritual, and said, "Look! This is *art*." It wasn't, of course. It was a fifteen-year-old girl's diary entry, meant for herself and not the world. There's a saying, loosely derived from Margaret Atwood, that men fear women will laugh at them, and women fear men will kill them. This is true. But we also fear laughter, for derision is a kind of slow death, one in which the self withers away to nothing, in which the hermit crab dies inside its shell.

What would I have had myself, or my peers, do differently? Certainly, I wish I had been stronger (or more talented), or less prone to depression, that I hadn't had to feel all of that hurt, or if I did, and I put it out there, and people laughed, that I was the kind of girl who could say "fuck you" in my head and move on.

What about my peers? How was my longtime crush supposed to react when he heard I had written a play about him in acting class, in which a teenage girl cares more about her unrequited crush than she does about her mother's recent death, other than with laughter? (Mr. Patch, dear Mr. Patch, one of the best grown-ups ever, had selected two of my classmates to act it out. He did it as a kindness to me, but I wish he hadn't.)

I would have laughed, had the situations been reversed. I too could be cruel. Kids often are. Adults too. It makes us uncomfortable to see someone so exposed, so unprotected. *Caring* so much. Perhaps I struggle now with expressing emotion not because I feel too little but because I feel too much. Because I *am* too much.

Sometimes, when writing in my journal, I address future historians. *I know you're there*, I often thought in the years I was writing this book, *and just to be clear, I know about what's going on. I know about the Nazis and the kids in cages and the police shootings and and and.* I don't want them to think I didn't know. I don't

Crosshatch

want them to think I cared only about myself. Scant information about anything but her personal life, the finding aid for my papers reads. Sometimes I'll tell them that: *I don't care only about my own suffering, so don't say that. You're doing history wrong. That's not what I mean. That's not what I mean at all.*

In a recent article for the *Journal of Women's History*, historian Kelly O'Donnell shares a series of delightful anecdotes about her research on the feminist health activist Barbara Seaman. While preparing to donate her papers to Harvard University's Schlesinger Library on the History of Women in America, Seaman wrote notes to researchers. According to O'Donnell, "in just about every box, there were post-it notes and scrawled messages on file folders, explicitly providing future researchers with clarification on certain matters and suggesting interpretation of her actions." In one, Seaman left a "note to all who believe that feminists neglected day care in the 1970s ... I didn't when I was Childcare & Education editor at *Family Circle* in 1970–73." "This is an historic letter," she began another message, appended to a letter from the secretary of the Department of Health, Education, and Welfare.[2]

My favorite notebook brand facilitates a similar kind of talking back. Each one comes with a table of contents at the beginning so writers can note the subjects they discuss on each page, as well as stickers to label the outside. This is very considerate to future historians. Everyone should do this. I probably won't, ADHD and all. But perhaps decades from now I'll go back and leave notes begging researchers not to be too hard on my younger self.

My current journal is nearly perfect, by the way, with a sturdy, vibrant teal cover and creamy pages that lie flat on my

---

2 Kelly O'Donnell, "The Activist Archive: Feminism, Personal-Political Papers, and Recent Women's History," *Journal of Women's History* 32, no. 4 (2020): 90, 91.

lap while I scribble. I would have preferred the purple one, but my favorite pen writes in purple ink, and it wouldn't do to be *so* matchy-matchy. The ink remains just visible when I turn the page; once it is full, my diagonal writing looks like crosshatch. Instead of lines there are dots, tiny stars peeking through the words. I spent too much money on it, especially considering all of the random old notebooks I have lying around – old drugstore spiral notebooks, novelty journals that as a teenager I thought were cute or funny. It really is lovely, though.

I know that, encountering this manuscript in the archive, I would do the same as those future historians, approaching my own writing as an academic encountering a primary document or a critic out for the next hot take. What a silly endeavor is this probing, this questioning. As if we can figure out *what they really meant* and, in the process, *who they really are.*

Once, on a whim, I processed and compiled a finding aid for my own papers. It's *seventeen pages long.* It must have been a form of procrastination, a way of avoiding the actual work of writing.

Then, too, I thought it might supplement my meager memories. It bothers me as a nonfiction writer of ostensibly personal narratives to remember so little. How do memoirists do it? How do they recreate, in detail, entire narratives from childhood? My brain does not work this way. Instead I have these papers, which cover such a small amount of time, only five or six years, and are so incomplete. Other sources, of course, abound: pictures, material artifacts, programs from school plays. But to access my inner life, this is all I have. I'm not sure if it's any more or less reliable than memories.

This exercise was also, strangely, a way of inserting myself in history, a way of imagining how historians would make sense out of my life decades from now. Perhaps, finally, they will be able to give some context to my life, to explain the

Crosshatch

bigger stories of which I am a part.

I started with Series I: Writing: Notebooks, 1997–2003, eight spiral-bound Mead five-subject notebooks. I used them for journaling, for poetry (more journaling, but with line breaks), for daily calorie counts and Andy Roddick fan fiction. "As long as I have pen and paper, I will not go crazy," I sometimes wrote over and over again. It's all suffused with so much *longing*, which simultaneously saddens, embarrasses, and amuses me, the same way watching an episode of *My So-Called Life* does. Please, *please* stop being so awkward, so raw and earnest, I beg my younger self. The notebooks are half full, a third full, only a few pages full, abandoned as soon as I mucked up the possibility of the blank page by somehow not being the person or the writer I wanted to be.

For years the notebooks sat in a box in the corner of my South Philly row home basement, which I always associated with memories, with the past, anyway. It smelled exactly like my grandparents' basement, like the grapes and plums and apples kept cool in the back room.

The bottom of the box was wet and disintegrating, leaving dirt and mold and cardboard detritus on the backs of several notebooks. The pages were waterlogged and stuck together and could not be easily read. A tiny silverfish ran across one of them, and I debated bringing them upstairs. The cats would eat anything. At the very least, they would enjoy eating the boxes.

Research is always embodied. Dust and mold give me a sore throat and a terrible headache. I forget about this discomfort every time I do archival work, and I spend all day wondering why I feel sick. I hate the feel of old paper, the way dust covers my hands, the way old newspapers feel almost fuzzy, like peach skin.

The deterioration of my materials was not intentional. I did not do it so that people could not read my words. How improbable, though, that anything is saved, that anything is adequately preserved. How improbable that anything would not disintegrate into dust.

I do this as a gift to you, future historians. Here is insight into white, middle-class teen girl culture at the turn of the millennium. Figure out whom I give pseudonyms in my other writing. Wonder what I destroyed, what I left to molder even longer in my basement.

This process gives me pause, though. I take notes from high school friends out of the notebooks where they have spent the last two and a half decades to put them in Series I: Writing: Correspondence, and I feel like I am doing something wrong. Archives take lives apart, and historians try to put them back together. The writing process is like that, too – assembling, taking apart, putting back together. Afternoons spent sitting on the floor of my office with scissors and Scotch tape. One can do that with text. But a life – once it's dissolved into its discrete, constitutive parts, can it ever be the same again?

Papers aren't a life, though. People's lives don't stop in between when they're producing documents. I need to remember that.

Research tricks you this way: "It captivates you, producing the sensation of having finally caught hold of the real, instead of looking through a 'narrative of' or 'discourse on' the real." The archive

> gives rise to the naïve but profound feeling of tearing away a veil, or crossing through the opaqueness of knowledge and, as if after a long and uncertain voyage, finally gaining access to the essence of beings and things. The archive lays things bare, and in a few crowded lines you can find not only the inaccessible but also the living. Scraps of lives dredged up from the depths wash up on shore before your eyes. Their clarity

Crosshatch

and credibility are blinding. Archival discoveries are a manna that fully justify their name: sources, as refreshing as wellsprings.[3]

Surely Martha exists in her journals, thinner than mine, with marbled, earth-toned covers. They're held together with string, softened from years of researchers tying and untying them. Presumably these journals didn't come with instructions for how to archive them. Presumably Martha didn't think about that.

Archives don't lie, but they don't tell the whole truth. Every finding aid has a shadow self, a nonfinding or unfinding aid that, if it existed, would list for researchers the documents that do not appear in a given collection. The archive is a record of absence. My unfinding aid lists all of the AOL chats that I didn't print out, all of the notes passed during homeroom that I didn't tuck into the folders in my notebooks, all of the thoughts I never committed to paper. What is in Martha's?

---

3 Farge, *The Allure of the Archives*, 7–8.

CHAPTER FIVE: CIVILIAN

Thousands of men rushed to enlist as soon as Lincoln issued his call for troops in April 1861. "I appeal to all loyal citizens," the president urged, "to ... aid this effort to maintain the honor, the integrity, and the existence of our National Union, and the perpetuity of popular Government; and to redress wrongs already long endured." Two years before the Battle of Gettysburg, war felt close already. Not all who responded were antislavery − for many Northerners, as for Lincoln, it was first about preserving the Union − though all of Martha's friends and family members were committed to the cause. Though many Quakers felt conflicted about the war, Martha herself was no pacifist; two years earlier, in 1859, she had mourned the death of abolitionist John Brown as a noble martyr. War was a terrible business but would be worth it if it ended with emancipation.[1]

Oldden Ridgway, one of Martha's closest friends, was among the new enlistees of spring 1861. It was another relationship that flummoxed observers. Their parents did not understand how they could be so intimate without being romantically involved. "We are just like brother and sister,"

1 Abraham Lincoln, "A Proclamation by the President of the United States," Apr. 15, 1861, US Capitol Visitor Center, https://www.visitthecapitol.gov/exhibitions/artifact/proclamation-president-united-states-april-15-1861.

Martha wrote.[2] They were even closer than that. In many ways, Oldden replaced the biological brother whom Martha rarely saw.

Oldden joined the First Infantry Division of the Pennsylvania Reserve Corps. In June he left with his rifle company for Camp Wayne in West Chester, twenty miles from Darby.

Martha had some idea of what camp life was like. A month earlier, she and Oldden had visited Suffolk Park in West Philadelphia, where over two thousand Ohio soldiers were encamped. Scarce provisions, hastily constructed shelter, all manner of men of whom she did not approve: all of this would soon be Oldden's. At least he had a blanket from his aunt to keep him warm.

"Poor fellow, I may never see him again," Martha wrote as he prepared to leave. When he said goodbye, he thanked Martha for her friendship, as if they would not meet again.[3]

By August his unit had set off for the South, though he hoped not for long. "A few more such blows" like the recent capture of forts in Roanoke, Virginia, and Bowling Green, Kentucky, "would I think pretty well wip them out," he wrote the following February. The mud was deep, the soldiers' tents dirty.[4]

Oldden was confident that Major General George B. McClellan could secure victory in the final phase of the Peninsula Campaign, a months-long Union offensive to capture the insurgent capital of Richmond and end the rebellion for good. His regiment saw heavy fighting in the Seven Days Battles, fought near Richmond in June and July of 1862. Facing a rebel army newly reorganized under General Robert E. Lee, Union forces inflicted heavy casualties but were eventually forced to retreat.

---

2 MS diary, May 26, 1861.
3 MS diary, May 5, 1861.
4 WOR to MS, Feb. 16, 1862.

Crosshatch

At night, as the battle raged on in Virginia, Martha and her family members read aloud to one another the names of dead and wounded soldiers. She dreaded to look for Oldden's name. During the school week, Martha passed her days in suspense, rushing as soon as she dismissed her students to buy a newspaper. She stood in the street and scanned the list of casualties as streetcars and people rushed by. Likely many others did the same. Perhaps her heart beat fast. Perhaps she raised a hand to her forehead. If she saw no names she recognized, she could go on with her day – run errands, gossip with a friend or sister on the car ride home. But Oldden stayed on her mind, especially when she was tending to the sick and wounded at the hospital. Their fate, or worse, could be his. Not until two weeks after the battle did she learn that he had emerged from five days of fighting uninjured.

In September 1862, after sixteen months away, Oldden returned to Darby. At home he did not speak of war.

Why don't thee tell some hair breathed escapes or some soldier's yarn? Martha asked. Oldden had briefly been captured by rebel soldiers and escaped. But it gave him no pleasure to speak of the battlefield, to which he would return as soon as he was well enough. He hoped the next generation would not romanticize war.[5]

November 27, 1862 was Thanksgiving. Martha and Oldden rode together to the hospital, where she and other volunteers had prepared a feast for the sick and wounded. She knew it might be their last carriage ride together: Oldden was scheduled to return to his regiment two days later. The food was plentiful and the crowd cheerful, but Martha knew that for many the happiness was an act. Hers certainly was. A dull, sad pain surrounded her.

Oldden was not her son, brother, or husband, but he was as dear to Martha as a family member. Perhaps he would not

5 MS to SB, Oct. 9, 1862.

survive; perhaps he would return permanently incapacitated in mind or body. At their last tea together, Martha had to leave the room several times to avoid breaking down in front of him. He must have noticed. It can't have been easy to comfort friends and family members while fearing death oneself.

On the night that Oldden left, Martha was sitting up with a badly burned neighbor child. As she tended to her patient, her thoughts wandered to her friend. She heard the whistle of the train as it bore him away.

* * *

Oldden survived the Peninsula Campaign, but others in Martha' life weren't so lucky. In June 1862, she learned that her seventeen-year-old cousin Joe Schofield had been killed in the Battle of Seven Pines, shot in the head as he reloaded and took aim. A lieutenant saw him fall.

He was one of the best in his regiment, Joe's colonel told the young man's father while relaying the news, *he did his part, bravely, heroically, nobly*.[6]

A flood the night before had left the roads muddy, and as members of the 104th Pennsylvania Regiment marched through the streets on the morning of May 31, 1862, their boots must have been heavy. For three hours, Joe's regiment faced enemy fire on its own. More than a third of its members fell before the entire group was forced to retreat.

The dead lay on the ground until June 2, when Confederate forces left the field. Captain Pickering and a small detail went looking for the dead of Company K, Joe's company, and buried all they found. Was Joe's body among these? Pickering likely did not know: "It was impossible to recognize many of the dead, the hot sun and rain had so disfigured their counte-

---

6 MS to SB, June 12, 1862.

Crosshatch

nances. Many of their faces had swollen up and burst."[7]

"I am tired of the sickening sight of the battlefield, with its mangled corpses & poor suffering wounded! Victory has no charms for me when purchased at such cost," General McClellan wrote to his wife after the battle.[8]

Martha remembered holding Joe on her lap when he was a baby. "My poor dear Cousin, only 17," she wrote. She wished someone had been there to hold him while he died. On the evening of Joe's death, Martha had written about the inevitability of mortality. She could not have known how timely it was.[9]

"Another tie is broken," Joe's father observed. His wife had died just two years earlier.[10]

Joe's death was not what nineteenth-century Americans considered a Good Death: a peaceful, acquiescent one surrounded by friends and family members. Civil War deaths inevitably thwarted this paradigm. Sometimes fellow soldiers, doctors, and nurses wrote to family members to reassure them of their loved one's Good Death. Sometimes witnesses let delirious men believe these onlookers really were the dying man's parents, wife, or siblings. But Joe's death was too sudden for even these accommodations. No one comforted him or listened to his last words.

Six months later, Martha visited her uncle. She was so used to seeing Joe there. She saw his photograph instead, covered in crepe and topped with a silk flag. Her uncle read aloud letters from Joe's colonel and captain, both full of praise. *He had always obeyed orders, no matter how distasteful*, one read. He had

---

7 Pickering quoted in W. W. H. *Davis, History of the 104th Pennsylvania Regiment, from August 22nd, 1861, to September 30th, 1864* (Philadelphia: Jas. B. Rodgers, 1866) 111.

8 McClellan quoted in *David J. Eicher, The Longest Night: A Military History of the Civil War* (New York: Simon & Schuster, 2001), 279.

9 MS to SB, June 20, 1862.

10 MS to SB, June 12, 1862.

been such a noble boy, Martha thought. At least he had died with a spotless soul.[11]

* * *

John was not among those who enlisted as soon as the war broke out. As postmaster he was exempt from the draft, and he adhered to the Quaker peace testimony.

"J. would rather go to prison than take up arms against a human being," Martha told Sadie.[12]

He was also not well in the summer and fall of 1862. He appeared to Martha thin and weak, and she worried he would not live long. He was a poor fit for military service.

By September, though, Philadelphia itself was in danger. Rebels had entered Maryland, and some had even trespassed into the free state of Pennsylvania. The authorities warned Philadelphia residents that the city could be invaded within a week. Stores closed at three in the afternoon, and hundreds left the city each day. Martha thought of fighting coming to Philadelphia or Darby – slightly to the west, and thus even closer to the rebel forces – and shuddered. "We know not how soon our own noble state will be invaded or in how little time the City of Brotherly Love, & the temple of the Declaration of Independence may be desecrated by the hands of traitors," she wrote.[13]

In one twenty-four-hour period, ten thousand Pennsylvania men volunteered for service. Sixty Darby men, including John, his brother, and state senator Jacob S. Serrill, formed a volunteer company to defend the state.

"It came like a shock to me," Martha wrote. John was so frail, so unsuited for a soldier's life. Martha had never

---

11 MS to SB, Jan. 20, 1863; MS to SB, June 12, 1862.

12 MS to SB, Aug. 5, 1862.

13 MS to SB, n.d. [Sept. 1862, mislabeled summer 1863].

Crosshatch

expected that he would abandon his pacifist principles. John did not see it that way, though.[14]

"When the Rebels found every man was rising up, they would stay away & it would prevent a battle," he told Martha.[15]

Martha thought about all of this as she watched the company train in the field across from her house.

"If they do go, my heart will be sick," she promised. She couldn't sleep even on the cool, quiet late summer nights.[16]

The men left for Harrisburg, then stood guard in sight of rebel pickets for almost thirty-six hours with nothing to eat. But the expected battle did not come in 1862; that would wait until the following year. The Darby men were demobilized after only two weeks and returned home, where their neighbors feted them with a celebratory dinner. John was sunburnt but well, and within three weeks he had started to regain his strength.

Martha confessed her feelings about John's military service in an undated letter fragment to Sadie. The finding aid dates this letter to summer 1863. At first glance this attribution makes sense; my first instinct when presented with a letter about an imminent invasion of Pennsylvania would be to place it just before the Battle of Gettysburg, but the letter is from September 1862, not 1863. Martha voiced the same concerns about John's health, his unsuitability for military service, and the threat of rebel invasion in her diary that month; a history of the Pennsylvania volunteers confirms that John's unit, the 16th Regiment, was organized on September 17, 1862, and disbanded on the twenty-fifth.

* * *

14 MS to SB, [Sept. 1862].
15 MS to SB, [Sept. 1862].
16 MS to SB, [Sept. 1862].

Oldden once insisted to Martha, "You at home know little of the effects of war. You would not know that war was going on but for the papers and the absent ones." But this isn't true at all. Martha had important things to do too.[17]

Back at home, news delayed, stomach roiling with fear, Martha did what she could. Collecting food for soldiers. Sewing garments for contraband, formerly enslaved persons who had escaped behind Union lines but whose legal status remained ambiguous. Producing goods to sell at Sanitary Fairs.

Nursing the sick and wounded at local hospitals.

"I cannot take up the sword or buckle or the armor for defense," she wrote, "perhaps I would not if I could." But "I do not see how the corps are to be gathered, unless, the Woman go to work."[18]

Louisa May Alcott traveled from Massachusetts to Washington, DC, to work in a soldiers' hospital. Martha did not need to leave home to do so; local hospitals treated thousands of young men from the front. At Summit House in West Philadelphia, Martha comforted men with bullet wounds and shattered limbs, typhoid, dysentery, and burns, reading to them to distract from the pain, serving them meals. Some were victims of an accident on the Baltimore Railroad: one man who had lost all of the skin from his hands another whose broken leg was amputated. Others came straight from battle. Surely some of them, as they went in and out of consciousness, mistook Martha for their sister, a role she knew well, or wife, one she never would. One young man, just eighteen, had lain in the field for several days with a bullet wound in his arm before medics transported him to the hospital. He died with his mother and siblings watching. They had said goodbye to him just two weeks before he was shot. Perhaps, watching him die, Martha thought of her cousin Joe.

17 WOR to Schofield, May 16, 1862.
18 MS to SB, Aug. 24, 1862, July 2, 1863.

Crosshatch

* * *

Martha did not, however, write about the war as much as one might expect. Sometimes her reticence derived from overwhelm. "I scarcely know how to begin to talk on paper about the times," she confessed early in the war, in May 1861. But it's also true that in certain ways her life didn't change all that much in these years, and I write about parts of her life that overlapped chronologically with the war in other chapters. I'm conflicted about this decision. Does it inflict violence on a life, to separate it out into parts like this, belying the way Martha experienced it? I worry, as I worried about separating out my papers. I frequently remind myself, as I did then, that this book is not a life. It is a story.[19]

Martha's relationship to the war was not unique. "During four years of Civil War," historians Paul Cimbala and Randall Miller note, "most Northerners conducted their lives as they had before Confederate forces had fired on Fort Sumter," though all of life's quotidian and remarkable aspects were inflected with anxiety. Life, somehow, goes on, as it must. But the fact that Martha's life — a woman's life — went on in this way is for me a feminist point.[20]

I do not *want* Martha's inner life to be subsumed by the capital-H History, the White Men Doing Important Things version of history, taking place. As the nation crumbled around her, she continued to insist that her thoughts and feelings — however small, however domestic — deserved attention. Because if we define history as a force that yanks us out of our daily lives, then history will never include people whose existence has often been defined by everydayness. It will never include, for example, most women.

---

19 MS to SB, May 10, 1861.
20 Paul A. Cimbala and Randall M. Miller, *The Northern Home Front during the Civil War* (Santa Barbara, CA: ABC-CLIO, 2017), xi.

Other women writers have treated war similarly. Martha's contemporary Louisa May Alcott focused in *Little Women* on the personal lives of four young women in the midst of upheaval. Emily Dickinson even managed to smuggle some of the most explicit menstrual imagery of the era into a poem about the Civil War, "The name – of it – is 'Autumn,'" putting women's daily struggles on the same level as nation-rending strife. True, the war was farther away in Massachusetts, where Alcott and Dickinson lived, than it was in Pennsylvania. So was slavery. But consider this: decades later, as the Battle of Britain raged overhead at the beginning of World War II, Virginia Woolf spent her days recalling her girlhood. "Yesterday (18th August 1940) five German raiders passed so close over Monks House," where she and her husband, Leonard, lived, "that they brushed the tree at the gate. But being alive today … I will go on with this loose story."[21]

There is something else, though: Alcott, Dickinson, Woolf, and Martha had much in common – commonalities that, taken together, made it easy for them to just keep living their lives.

* * *

But I'll go on with this loose story, which brings us to Gettysburg. In the spring of 1863, war was very close to Philadelphia. On moonlit nights, the Darby company trained in the field across from Martha's house, as they had done the previous fall. She could hear the drums beat as the soldiers marched. In July, Union and rebel forces met at Gettysburg, a day's ride from Darby. Convalescent patients left the hospital to rejoin their regiments, and Oldden and John prepared to go too. No longer postmaster and newly susceptible to the

---

21 Woolf, "A Sketch of the Past," 124.

Crosshatch

draft, John had registered in June. He wrote to his militia captain asking to rejoin the company. Oldden, his health still poor, had been discharged in January, but he felt duty-bound to go.

The city was not prepared, though its residents planned to build fortifications. Martha was ready to experience any suffering that strengthened the nation's cause.

Summit House admitted six hundred men from the battlefield, only a fraction of those taken to area hospitals. John's younger brother Will, then seventeen or eighteen, was shot in the arm and taken to another hospital in West Philadelphia. Phil Price, the brother of Martha's uncle, was shot in the foot and brought home for his relatives to care for him.

Less than two weeks later, an ugly coda: in New York City, resentful working-class whites rampaged through the city, attacking the homes of Black Americans and their white abolitionist allies and burning the Colored Orphan Asylum to the ground. Union troops, already exhausted from battle, had to march over two hundred miles from Gettysburg to quell the riots, which resulted in over a hundred deaths.

At night, Martha called out to Sadie in Brooklyn, so close to the riots. *Sadie, Sadie, my child, my friend, where art thou, O answer me, that I may go to sleep in peace.*[22]

Gettysburg is the expected climax to any Civil War narrative set in Pennsylvania, but any diaries Martha kept between February 1863 and June 1864 are lost. Historical sources abound on the battle itself; I can learn about it in other ways. I want to know something quite different: when Martha learned, and how she felt when she found out, that her best friend was okay. Not White Men Doing Important Things. I'll leave that to others. I know they've got it covered. Show me instead the small, secret moments in people's lives, the hopes and fears and loves that even war could not subsume.

22 MS to SB, July 15, 1863.

Christina Larocco

* * *

"Bad news," a neighbor announced when he appeared at the Schofield-Child family's window early in the morning of April 15, 1865. Lincoln had been shot the night before and died just hours ago.[23] What could Martha say in the face of such epochal, unimaginable events? "No words of mine can describe these days of horror and sorrow," Martha wrote the day that Lincoln died; two days later, "no words can express the deep feelings every where;" two days after that, any writing "would be little to the reality."

> My feelings could not find vent in words.
> Words seem weak.
> Words fail me.[24]

Grief consumed Martha, but so did anger: at John Wilkes Booth, at the Southern insurgents, at their Northern Copperhead sympathizers. All were culpable. Inside she burned, dreaming of revenge. Death to all of the rebel leaders would not be too severe a punishment.

Philadelphia had been preparing for a victory celebration. Days before, Robert E. Lee had surrendered to Ulysses S. Grant at Appomattox Court House in Virginia, and the city was to be illuminated as never before. Instead, the streets were silent. Black crepe covered houses and public buildings, and all stores and shutters were closed. Newspaper boys hawked their goods in silence. Thousands were in the streets, silent faces bearing the mark of sorrow.

After his funeral in Washington, Lincoln's body journeyed to his birthplace of Springfield, Illinois, traveling through Philadelphia and several other American cities on its way.

23 MS to SB, Apr. 24, 1865.
24 MS diary, Apr. 15, 17, 19, 1865; MS to SB, Apr. 24, 1865.

Crosshatch

Eight horses pulled the sixteen foot–high hearse down Broad Street, followed by a parade so long it took two hours for it to pass by. By the time the parade reached Martha and her family, it was dark, the marchers illuminated by gas.

The next day, Martha and her family left Darby just after five in the morning. to see the body. The line stretched for miles. Martha waited four-and-a-half hours to get into Independence Hall, where Lincoln's coffin lay covered in mourning cloth, surrounded by flowers and shrouded portraits of famous Americans. Carpeting muffled any sounds. The Liberty Bell stood at the head of the coffin, which as many as eighty thousand people passed by. Martha did so twice: once with her mother and stepfather, once with her sister Lydia.

It was dark by the time she and Lydia made it into the hall, and candles illuminated Lincoln's waxen face. Officials hurried them through, and she secured only a glance. It was just as well, though. She preferred to remember him alive, to recreate, as best she could, the moments before she knew what was going to happen.

Interlude: The Museum of Human History

In my youth, when I thought about difficult periods in history – war, economic upheaval, public health crises – I often wondered how people endured. Four years of Civil War, a decade of depression. How did they survive, how did they face each day knowing that it was going to last for *so long*? The answer, of course, is that they didn't know.

How would I have felt in March 2020 if someone had told me how long the pandemic would last? It would have been unimaginable at that point. Unbearable. Wall-kickingly, hair-tearingly unbearable.

Robert E. Lee surrendered at Appomattox Court House in April 1865, but in many important ways the Civil War never ended. It seems clear now that the pandemic has affected our social fabric so deeply that it will never end, either. Someday people will feel as if they were born knowing this, just like I can't imagine not knowing what happened to Lincoln, like I can't imagine not knowing that Darth Vader is Luke's father, or that Romeo and Juliet die, or that Dr. Jekyll and Mr. Hyde are the same person.

* * *

I can't write the Civil War the way Martha lived it. So much of history – by which I mean not the past itself but the study thereof, the way we understand it – is dramatic irony. I don't know how, as a historian, to capture the sense of not-knowing, of not-narrative, that I experience in my own life, with stories and shapes that emerge only after the fact. That's not exactly true: we impose stories on our lives even as we are living them. But the words we use to describe these stories reveal a particular understanding of history, and especially of how our own lives fit into it, or, more to the point, how they *don't*.

It's easy in Philadelphia to feel the slippage between the past and the present. A morning spent transcribing a letter about viewing Lincoln's body in Independence Hall becomes an evening walking past the landmark to get noodles in Chinatown. If anyplace manifests history's ubiquity, if anyplace can remind me that history surrounds us, this is it. Still, until recently, until I had nearly finished this book, in fact – I struggled to believe, deep down, that these events *really happened*.

Because if history happened once, it could happen again.

And, if we're wise, there's little of history that we should want to live through.

But let me go back two decades, to when I first realized I was living through history: the incomprehensibility with which that hit me. Once, as a child, Ashley and I (Ashley of the princess adventures, the excursions that tethered me to home even as I tried to escape it) tried to surf down the snowy back hill of my childhood home, standing on our sleds. I fell, of course, and for what felt like minutes no breath circulated in my body. I thought I was dying. It was the only time that I have felt physically the slow-motion psychic trauma of this realization.

Perhaps it began on November 8, 2000, the day after the first election in which I voted. My roommates and I walked back to our dorm room from the dining hall to find that Al Gore, the Democratic candidate and current vice president,

Crosshatch

had retracted his concession from the night before. A recount began. We did not know who the next president was going to be.

"Wow, this is, like, historic," Joanna said.

"Well, every presidential election is historic," Melissa, another roommate, replied.

"No, but, I mean, like – this is *historic*."

I knew what Joanna meant. To her, to me, "historic" meant something so far outside of our experience, so far from our understanding of what the world was like, that it seemed to belong to the past, a time when *real things* happened. Only by seeing these events as history could we make any sense out of them.

In the blink of an eye, it was sixteen years later, on the eve of another election, eerie light shining through the arches of Independence Hall as Bruce Springsteen played a melancholy acoustic version of "Dancing in the Dark." This, too, felt historic.

By which I mean: unreal, surreal, or somehow *too real*.

By which I mean: unrelated to me or my life, its small, ho-hum everydayness.

And therein lies the problem, because who is allowed to feel this way? Only a person to whom the next day mattered greatly emotionally but little concretely, a person whose life would most likely not change tremendously regardless of the outcome. Alcott, Dickinson, Woolf, and Martha. Me.

* * *

History, though, can happen to anyone, anywhere. I was unprepared when it did. In the fall of 2001, my sophomore year of college, I wrote a poem about the US going to war. Even before I processed my papers, when my archive was made up of copy paper boxes full of journals and stories and plays moldering in my basement, this particular document was conveniently located in a folder full of other writing from the fall, as it should be. Amid era-defining events, I could only envision myself as a film heroine missing her boyfriend in some vaguely-World-War-II-ish-but-also-kind-of-Vietnam-era past. The past, when *real things* happened. The past, which in my nineteen-year-old mind all happened at the same time.

> If this truly is what it is, what
> everyone says it is, then I
> need a red lipstick, a
> good red lipstick that is
> pure and
> true and
> rich and
> enduring,
> a lipstick that goes
> well with knee-length wool
> skirts and soft, wavy
> hair and
> rationed stockings with seams and
> perfume to spray on replies
> to tattered, censored letters.
>
> I need a box
> to keep my heart in
> and a necklace from a boy
> who left for Canada
> long, elegant fingers I can
> file as I
> answer the phone and bring
> messages to my boss who
> smokes cigars and rolls up his shirt-sleeves,
> smacking me on the behind and

Crosshatch

saying, "thanks, honey"
as I leave his office.

I need a pair of two-inch
heels, stacked, with a shiny silver
buckle, that clack when I
walk and draw the collective gaze of
bell-bottomed sailors on leave
elongate my calves
dig into my ankles
give me blisters on my toes and
don't provide enough support for my
fallen arches and
yes,
I, too, feel pain.

Pretty good for nineteen, right?

Several years ago, when a colleague of mine was teaching at West Point, a student asked her when an event became part of history. My colleague paused, then suggested that it was when young people no longer remembered an event that was central to older generations' identities.

"Oh, like 9/11?" the student responded. An old *Onion* article bears the headline "18-Year-Old Fighting in Afghanistan Has 9/11 Explained to Him by Older Soldier." For years younger colleagues have asked me, "What's the big deal? There are terrorist attacks all the time." Most Gen Zers, including those who are now the age I was then, were not yet born. What do they care?

Indeed, it's hard sometimes to remember what the big deal was. For stretches of 2021, more Americans died of COVID *each day* than died on 9/11. "The 9/11 Era Is Over," declared a slew of think pieces in late 2020 and early 2021, and this certainly seems true. What does this mean for those of us whose identities so fundamentally reflect that event? Are Millennials ranting about George W. Bush now the Baby Boomers who won't stop talking about the Sixties, our minds and bodies archives of a bygone era?

I remember how disconcerting it was when all of a sudden, the early aughts had a recognizable aesthetic: those blonde highlights, those low-rise jeans. "Her eyebrows are *so* 2002," I often find myself saying while watching old episodes of *Buffy the Vampire Slayer*. It's become an *era*, is what I mean – and an era that is now over.

How inexorable it all is. I didn't know.

I was just shy of twenty then; Martha turned twenty-two in the months before the rebels fired on Fort Sumter. Everything had changed, or so it seemed, and I didn't know how to make sense out of it. "I am living history," I wrote in my journal, but it felt equally like a movie. "I keep waiting for this to be over, for the credits to roll so I can walk out of the theatre and get back to my normal life." I didn't know about simulacra then.

Recently my father asked me if I wanted a printed batch of emails we had written to each other while I was in college, that liminal period between the material and the digital.

"YES!" I said. He was surprised. Into the archive they went.

I remember one of these emails. He wrote: "I'm so sorry, Christina. I had hoped that nothing like this would ever be a part of your life."

So that one I don't have to look up. It's not so much that I trust my memory as much as I trust documentation – though in this case I do; how strange to admit that – as it is that I just can't bear to look at it. Usually, for me, research is something to hide behind, a way to avoid the painful and the personal, but in this case it's just the opposite. I'm so eager to go through other people's papers, to discover their deepest,

Crosshatch

darkest secrets. Yet I can't look at mine.

Back in my dorm room, Joanna and Melissa and I drank and ate ice cream. My email inbox flooded with messages from high school friends, aunts and uncles and cousins. *Are you okay?* They all asked. I responded to them all and then put up a simple away message: *I am okay.* I wanted everyone to know, and I was lucky that I could tell them far more quickly than Sadie could tell Martha after the draft riots. I chatted with friends on AOL Instant Messenger, my typing getting sloppier and sloppier.

"Do you want me to come over to cuddle?" a boy asked me that night on IM. Neither of our buildings had been evacuated. As other students, unable to return to their buildings farther south, huddled on the floor of the athletic center, we could still sleep in our beds. It couldn't hurt to huddle together there, too. I kind of thought this boy had a crush on me and kind of thought he wasn't interested in girls. I had been sick all summer and was skinny, finally skinny, so I suppose I thought it had to be one or the other. But I was drunk, and this boy hated talking to people when they were drunk.

People reacted in all sorts of ways. Two days later I was in Wantaugh, Long Island, walking on the beach with Joanna and her terrible boyfriend, Joe. She was crying, and he was yelling at her for making too big of a deal out of it. Two of my other roommates got into a big fight a few days later. One of them had written in a class assignment that she had returned home the night of 9/11 to find the rest of us putting on makeup and preparing to go out, which wasn't true. She was blonde and pretty, one of those girls who would wear fairy wings to class. She had a handsome Welsh boyfriend, and everyone thought she was adorable. Wasn't that enough for her?

The epigraph to *The Things They Carried*, Tim O'Brien's gutting collection of interrelated, semiautobiographical stories about the Vietnam War, draws from the diary of John Ransom, an American soldier held by rebels at the notorious Andersonville, Georgia, prison camp. "This book," it reads, "is essentially different from any other that has been published concerning the 'late war' or any of its incidents. Those who have had any such experience as the author will see its truthfulness at once, and to all other readers it is commended as a statement of actual things by one who experienced them to the fullest." O'Brien's own book, he seems to tell us, will be very different: one in which fact and fiction are inextricable, muddy; one in which truth is so slippery that, perhaps, readers should not even bother searching for it. The collection's most famous piece, "How to Tell a True War Story," enacts this slippage explicitly.[1]

Yet Americans who experienced the Civil War may have found much familiar in O'Brien's account of events that took place a century later. Writers like Emily Dickinson, Herman Melville, and Ambrose Bierce – along with ordinary Americans – found that they could not understand or describe what they had witnessed; the Civil War challenged their understanding of truth, language, and the relationship between them. "The real war will never get in the books," Walt Whitman promised of the Civil War.[2] As Cornelia Hancock noted of nursing wounded soldiers after the Battle of Gettysburg, "There are no words in the English language to express the sufferings I witnessed today."[3] O'Brien used as a marker of pre-Vietnam truth something that its witnesses would not

---

1 John Ransom's Civil War Diary quoted in Tim O'Brien, *The Things They Carried* (Boston: Houghton Mifflin, 1990), epigraph.

2 Walt Whitman, "The Real War Will Never Get in the Books," in *Complete Prose Works* (Philadelphia: David McKay, 1892), 80.

3 Cornelia Hancock to cousin, July 7, 1863, in Hancock, *South after Gettysburg: Letters of Cornelia Hancock from the Army of the Potomac, 1863–1865*, ed. Henrietta Stratton Jaquette (1937; repr., Freeport, NY: Books for Libraries Press, 1971), 7.

Crosshatch

have understood that way. It's all shadows dancing on cave walls.

* * *

It is thus ironic but not surprising that for most of my life, O'Brien's era was the referent. As a teenager in the 1990s, I felt like I had missed out on the 1960s. Based on the fashions I saw in *Seventeen* and the *Delia's* catalogue, I was not the only one who felt this way. Girls my age wore bell bottoms and peasant blouses, styling ourselves after what seemed real and true.

Nothing in our youth prepared us for the onslaught of the twenty-first century, even though signs were everywhere for anyone who cared to look. Rodney King and Columbine, Timothy McVeigh. Our own Millennial "We Didn't Start the Fire." Had I paid attention, I might not have been so gobsmacked by the events to come.

"We came to New York because this is where real things happen," my friend Catherine said shortly after 9/11.

"Something was actually happening," says postmodern girl hero Angela Chase at the end of the first episode of *My So-Called Life*, "but it was too actual."

In *Simulacra and Simulation*, theorist Jean Baudrillard argues that we live in a state of hyperreality, "a real without origin or reality." We make sense out of our lives only through referents that are themselves illusions: this feels like a movie. I can only understand my life in terms of the past. But how can the same event feel simultaneously "like a movie" and historic? "History," writes Baudrillard, "is our lost referential, that is to say our myth." Perhaps, as Jacques Derrida might suggest, history is not something we experience at all but something that is constructed later. I never experienced the past not because I was born too late, but because it never existed: the past is a simulacrum. But what is a historian if not someone who tries to insert themselves into stories that were being told – whether or not they actually happened – long before they were born?[4]

"Do any human beings ever realize life while they live it?" Thornton Wilder's Emily asks in Act III of *Our Town*. It's the wrong question. We're perfectly aware of life, its intricate tedium. It's history we're unaware of, because it doesn't exist while we're living it – and thus, in a sense, it doesn't exist at all.[5]

* * *

As a child and adolescent, I'm sorry to say, my worldview in certain ways resembled no one's as much as Francis Fukuyama, one of the architects of neoconservatism. In a 1989 article for *The National Interest* and a book three years later, Fukuyama argued that the end of the Cold War also meant the end of history: with communism petering out, no significant challengers to Western liberal democracy and free-market capitalism remained. In the near future lay the "unabashed victory of economic and political liberalism" and the "universalization of Western liberal democracy as the final form of human government."[6]

"Without the Cold War, what's the point of being an American?" John Updike asked in *Rabbit at Rest*. "We thought the [Berlin] wall would stand forever," Yitzhak similarly tells the audience in *Hedwig and the Angry Inch*, "and now that it's gone, we don't know who we are anymore." A friend told me that, as a child in the 1980s, she always rooted – in the

---

4 Jean Baudrillard, *Simulacra and Simulation*, trans. Sheila Faria Glaser (Ann Arbor: University of Michigan Press, 1994), 43.

5 Thornton Wilder, *Our Town* (1938; repr., New York: Harper Perennial, 2003), 108.

6 Francis Fukuyama, "The End of History?" *The National Interest*, Summer 1989, 4.

Crosshatch

absence of any Americans – for Soviet athletes in the Olympics. She felt sorry for them, she explained. Even for those of us born in the last gasps of the Cold War, it provided a ready-made narrative, a convenient way to understand our place in the world, Reagan's "evil empire" speech practically a lullaby sung to us in our cribs.

Fukuyama's insistence on the end of history is ridiculous, of course, and he has rightly been criticized ever since for his chauvinist teleology. Today he no longer believes his own theory. "Twenty-five years ago," he told the *Washington Post* shortly after Trump's inauguration, "I didn't have a sense or a theory about how democracies can go backward. And I think they clearly can."[7]

In the years between the end of the Cold War and Trump's election, however, Fukuyama often felt his argument was misunderstood. He did not mean there would be no more events. He did not mean there would be no more conflicts. He meant that the ideological struggles of the past – most recently against fascism and communism – would no longer take place on a large scale; no longer would nation-states assert the superiority of their way of life; no longer would the bipolar antagonisms of the twentieth century define how nations thought about themselves and their role in the world. When he talked about the end of history, he was talking, I think, about the end of story: history as the hero's journey. For that reason, I feel some sympathy for Fukuyama, especially reading the moving and surprising final paragraph of his original piece:

> The end of history will be a very sad time. The struggle for recognition, the willingness to risk one's life for a purely abstract goal, the worldwide ideological struggle that called for daring, courage, imagination, and idealism, will be

---

7 Fukuyama cited in Ishaan Tharoor, "The Man Who Declared the 'End of History' Fears for Democracy's Future," *Washington Post*, Feb. 9, 2017.

replaced by economic calculations, the endless solving of technical problems, environmental concerns, and the satisfaction of sophisticated consumer demands. In the post-historical period there will be neither art nor philosophy, just the perpetual caretaking of the museum of human history. I can feel in myself, and see in others around me, a powerful nostalgia for the time when history existed. Such nostalgia, in fact, will continue to fuel competition and conflict in the post-historical world for some time to come … Perhaps this very prospect of centuries of boredom at the end of history will serve to get history started once again.[8]

This, too, is ridiculous, though perhaps not *wrong*, exactly: misguided nostalgia has driven the resurgence of right-wing populism in the US and western Europe. I can't pretend not to have spent much of my life feeling a similar nostalgia. Perhaps it is the reason I became a historian, the reason I am a writer: to get as close as I could to something I felt had passed me by.

Anyway, if Francis Fukuyama and Jean Baudrillard had a daughter, she would be a certain kind of oblivious teenage girl in the 1990s, privileged enough to come to the absurd conclusion that she missed everything. It's a profoundly conservative insistence, but I believed *so* strongly that there were no more epic stories to be a part of.

* * *

By the time I was old enough to be aware of big events, they didn't feel any realer than everyday life. They felt, rather, *surreal*. Merriam-Webster chose "surreal" as its Word of the Year in 2016, for relatively banal reasons: "It was looked up significantly more frequently by users in 2016 than it was in previ-

8 Fukuyama, "The End of History?" 18.

Crosshatch

ous years, and ... there were multiple occasions on which this word was the one clearly driving people to their dictionary." As Jonathan P. Eburne notes in a blog post for the *Los Angeles Review of Books*, "Since 9/11, the popular sense of the word 'surreal' has become a shorthand way to describe events that overwhelm our very sense of the world." *It was too actual*, the same reason Joanna had described the 2000 election as historic, the same reason 9/11 felt like a movie.

But if neither everyday life nor national tragedies felt real, what, exactly, did I think reality *was*? The answer, of course, is secret answer C: an Anthropologie catalogue.

Perhaps these feelings are just garden-variety existentialism. They're not so different from what Simone de Beauvoir described in a 1965 interview:

> ... the paradox of human life is precisely that one tries to *be* and, in the long run, merely exists. It's because of this discrepancy that when you've laid your stake on being – and, in a way, you always do when you make plans, even if you actually know that you can't succeed in being – when you turn around and look back on your life, you see that you've simply existed. In other words, life isn't behind you like a solid thing ... Your life is simply a human life.[9]

Twenty-five years earlier, Virginia Woolf labeled these parts of life "non-being," "a kind of nondescript cotton wool" that coats the day and the brain. "Every day," she noted near the end of her life, "includes much more non-being than being ... A great part of every day is not lived consciously. One walks, eats, sees things, deals with what has to be done; the broken

---

9 Simone de Beauvoir interviewed by Madeleine Gobeil, 1965, in *Women at Work: Interviews from the Paris Review*, vol. 1 (New York: Paris Review Editions, 2017), 64.

vacuum cleaner; ordering dinner; writing orders to Mabel; washing; cooking dinner; bookbinding." Non-being wasn't *bad*, exactly; a pleasant if forgettable lunchtime conversation with Leonard was surely *better* than a close call with German raiders. Still, "when it is a bad day the proportion of non-being is much larger."[10]

Laundry to be done. Groceries to buy. Boredom punctuated by terror. There's something to say, or a lot to say, for the kinds of lives that are allowed to exist in this state of non-being, which seems more than anything to be characterized by safety.

* * *

When I was in middle school, my favorite history teacher asked us to interview three relatives who were old enough to remember Vietnam. I chose my grandfather, my father, and my uncle: a World War II veteran and two of his four then–draft age sons. They had *lived*. They had experienced *history*. I don't remember much of what they said, except that my uncle didn't mind Jane Fonda's antiwar activism because she made sexy movies.

It never occurred to me to interview my grandmother, though it was she who had designed my father's draft-avoidance plan. I didn't know that then. When I taught, I sometimes had my students conduct oral history interviews. They, too, always chose their fathers or grandfathers, never their mothers or grandmothers. When I asked why, they said it was because these women's lives had been boring.

What a terrible time, I thought as I listened to the stories shared by the men in my family. So much death, so much strife. But deep, deep down in my wormy brain, I also thought: *How exciting*. I also thought: *I wish I had lived then.*

10 Woolf, "A Sketch of the Past," 70.

Crosshatch

Then it was 2001, then 2016. Then 2020. I had been doing all right, considering the circumstances, sad and scared for the world but trudging along myself. My equanimity failed me just weeks into the pandemic, when the Liacouras Center at Temple University became a makeshift hospital for COVID patients.

On March 28, Philadelphia mayor Jim Kenney announced that the city had reached an agreement to lease facilities, most notably the indoor basketball stadium, from the school at no cost. A space where bodies performed seemingly impossible feats of athletic prowess in front of some ten thousand fans would become a place where up to 250 bodies would struggle to stay alive. The *Philadelphia Inquirer* described the transformation this way:

> The area floor of Temple University's cavernous Liacouras Center is lined with hospital cots that sit below banners touting basketball championships. A cluster of wheelchairs sits by the loading dock, next to a concessions sign advertising Miller Lite specials. The electronic signs at the will-call box office are still blinking with reminders to "please show your ID," but the only people regularly coming into the arena these days are the workers who helped transform Temple's campus arena into a field hospital this weekend.[11]

Over the course of that year and the next, Americans learned more and more about how Black Americans were disproportionately affected by COVID. The last time I had been in the Liacouras Center before the pandemic was to hear Ta-Nehisi Coates speak. One of his themes was the way racism writes

---

11 Aubrey Whelan, "How Temple's Liacouras Center Was Transformed into a Hospital Site for the Coronavirus Pandemic," *Philadelphia Inquirer*, Mar. 30, 2020.

itself on the body.

It was the picture that got me: rows and rows of cots in a big open space, brisk efficiency in the face of chaos. Alone but exposed, patients' pain would be on full display.

I had seen this image before. It was the image of a Civil War hospital, the kind where Walt Whitman visited his wounded brother, where cholera and infected bullet wounds posed equal threats. The kind where Martha worked. Even sewing circles reappeared, as regular Americans made masks for healthcare workers and later themselves. COVID became real to me the moment it started to remind me of history. This timing does not surprise me.

In the end, the temporary hospital never needed to admit more than five or six patients at a time. It shut down a month after it opened. But in August 2021, the number of American COVID deaths topped the number of Civil War deaths – a staggering 620,000 individuals. It continued to rise for a long time.

* * *

While I was writing this book, I read an article by Szczepan Twardoch, a Polish author almost exactly my age. "I am 40 years old and not used to history," he writes in "History Is No Longer a Circle, Nor Is Progress Guaranteed": "History has not touched my life, not burned its frightening brand onto it. Frightening because when others are branded, that isn't history, but events." Events only become history when we can ascribe meaning to them, he seems to say, and much of what he has witnessed happening to others seems to have no meaning.

It's reminiscent of both Fukuyama's argument and the way I felt for the first two decades of my life, and intermittently thereafter. It's not a way that I can feel anymore. Whatever history is, I've experienced it.

Crosshatch

Like everyone, I reread *The Handmaid's Tale* shortly after the 2016 election. It's still great, of course, but I also found it hilarious how often Margaret Atwood used the "we never thought about [X], then" sentence structure. The comma in particular made me laugh. So dramatic. Four years later, in 2020, I joked along with everyone else about someday having to explain restaurants, live sports, and theater to my then-one-year-old nephew, Leo. We talked about the Before Times, but always as if it was partially a joke, partially in quotation marks. Irony protected us from living history too fully.

But truly, what will Leo ask me about this time, when his own history teacher asks him to interview people old enough to remember 2020? Surely I will seem like the perfect person to ask. *What was life like during the pandemic, Aunt Nina?*

What will I tell him? Will I tell him what I would have wanted to hear about the past? Or will I tell him the truth — that I experienced it more than anything as an overwhelming boredom, a fog that never completely lifted? Perhaps I will not be able to tell him the truth, even if I may have wanted to, if narrative and mythmaking have clouded my already fuzzy memories of those undifferentiated days to the point that it is impossible to tell a true pandemic story. No wonder people tell me that history is boring. Living it often is, at least. Yet the hardest truth to admit is that sometimes, now that it no longer feels like we are living through history, I wish we could go back. Will I tell him that?

CHAPTER SIX: BRIDESMAID

Weddings were on Martha's mind in 1859, the year she turned twenty. "Nature is arrayed in her bridal garment," she remarked of the year's first storm, "the pure white snow has fallen gently, and clothed every thing in angels dress." In May, her mother, widowed since Martha's early adolescence, married local doctor John Child. In September, Martha was a bridesmaid in her cousin Hannah F. Wilson's wedding to Guy Roberts.[1]

To Hannah's chagrin, rumors about the wedding had spread for almost a year. She had a difficult choice to make: Guy's business would soon bring him to California, and a decision to marry him was also a decision to leave her family and friends far behind. At thirty-one, Hannah was not young, but Guy was already in his sixties. Hannah would almost certainly find herself a young widow. Was love, in all its uncertainty, all its inevitable transience, worth it? Martha thought so:

> Thee knows dear in this world we must not cause anymore sorrow than we can help, and I am fully convinced that if thee did not accept that invitation, thee would make a sorrowing hart; you think of it; a "certain person" being all alone in a far off country,

1 MS diary, Jan. 4, 1859.

with no one but strangers; no one to sympathize in his joys; or console him in sadness; no one at whom he can pour forth his aspirations, none even who could suit him in doing up shirts and collars, although I have no interest in him, when I think of all these things, of all the sad hours he must spend while on his every journey, I feel heartfelt pity for his lonely condition.[2]

Am I surprised to find her such a romantic? Not in 1858, no, before so many disappointments.

Hannah eventually agreed. She and Guy received approval from their meeting in August 1859 and married the next month.

The plan did not leave much time to prepare, especially for Martha and the other two bridesmaids; in fact she heard about her appointment only through gossip. "When I am going to be married," she chided Hannah gently, "I will try to let you know at least I will give you time to think about it." In her next letter, she explained to Hannah that the reference to her own upcoming nuptials was a joke. It was neither the first nor the last time she would have to clarify in this way.[3]

The wedding was small even by Quaker standards, with some sixty guests, thirty-five of whom stayed overnight at Green Lawn Farm. It was beautiful, too, with a table full of cakes, ice cream, jellies, and other desserts brought from Philadelphia. The groomsman with whom Martha was paired

2 MS to Hannah F. Wilson, Nov. 10, 1858, in Frederick, *Dear Hannah*, 255. Frederick's volume conflates Martha Schofield, the subject of this book, with her first cousin Martha Ann Schofield (1840–1907). Their respective fathers, Oliver W. (1806–1852) and Jonathan T. Schofield (1811–79) were brothers; Martha Ann was thus also the older sister of Joe Schofield, who died in 1862 at the Battle of Seven Pines. Internal evidence, such as the location from which letters were postmarked, makes it clear which letters are relevant here.

3 MS to Hannah F. Wilson, Aug. 19[?], 1859, in Frederick, *Dear Hannah*, 294.

Crosshatch

and who waited on her at the reception was a good friend. Martha had fun with him and the rest of the bridal party, who remained for several days after the wedding. Among their outings was a lovely, moonlit carriage ride. But Martha had to leave for home sooner than she had originally planned.

Hannah's wedding, it turned out, was a rehearsal for Martha. Not for her own: oh, no. Just a month later, her sister Sallie married, the only one of the four sisters to do so. Martha rushed home from Hannah's wedding to prepare. There was so much sewing to be done, including Sallie's wedding dress.

Martha loved her brother-in-law, Samuel Ash, and she loved Sallie and Samuel's son, Howard, whom she often cared for after his birth a year later. Still, the marriage saddened her. "It will seem like loosing her," she wrote. Several months after the wedding, Sallie's twin, Lydia, still found it "very hard to realize even yet that she is married. I miss her so much. I often feel a great blank without her."[4]

Sallie's four bridesmaids wore silk. "Mine is very dark," Martha remarked, "as I wanted It for services afterwards." She was practical. But she also felt somber. "She is gone," she thought when the ceremony was over. Listening to Sallie and Samuel say their vows had been agony.[5]

The members of the wedding party wore white flowers. Against her dark dress, Martha's must have popped.

Less than a month later, Martha's sister Lydia accompanied her to the barber, who "cut my hair all off ... just like a boy." Perhaps it was a way of rebelling against heteronormative femininity, which must end in marriage. But she didn't like this haircut, uneven and impossible to style, either.[6]

4 MS to SB, Oct. 16, 1859; MS diary, Nov. 9, 1859; Lydia A. Schofield to Hannah F. Roberts, Feb. 27, 1860, in Frederick, *Dear Hannah*, 302. Oliver Howard Ash (1860–74) was named for his maternal grandfather but called Howard.
5 MS diary, Nov. 9, 1859.
6 MS diary, Nov. 11, 1859.

***

Martha met Sarah (Sadie) Mott Brouwer in November 1858, when Sadie joined Martha's class at the Willets Seminary in Harrison, New York. Sadie lived in Brooklyn with her mother and father, a rather dissolute businessman. "Another new scholar Sarah Brouwer, her Aunt & Uncle here to dine," Martha told her diary. She was nineteen, so young to be a teacher. Sadie, fifteen, was a "lovely creature." She was lonely and homesick, but Martha was kind to her. They would be friends, Martha told Sadie, and Martha would take care of her. Both women stayed with the Willets at their home. It was quiet on the weekends, when the other students went home to their families. The house was cozy, conducive to long, drowsy afternoons spent reading to each other and braiding each other's hair. *Jane Eyre* was one of their favorites.[7]

The few historians who have written about Martha have tried to write *Jane Eyre* onto her life, suggesting that she, too, fell in love with her employer, with whom she lived. It's less than convincing, though I understand the temptation.

Martha loved the Brontës, or at least Charlotte, whose heroines were more practical and romances less gothic than Emily's. Martha was Jane Eyre, not Cathy; as much as she loved nature, she could not have identified with a wild child of the moors as much as with a prim and proper governess.

What I don't understand is how Martha saw *Jane Eyre* as romantic, as anything other than the story of a cruel man who incarcerated his discarded, mentally ill first wife and the pious young woman willing to sacrifice her own self to take care of him. Perhaps it was the sacrifice itself that appealed to Martha. This is what seems to have drawn her to Charlotte Brontë as a person, at least: that "sensitive, shrinking nature"

---

7 MS diary, Nov. 9, 13, 1858, Mar. 23, 1859, box 1, folder correspondence, 1858–1859.

Crosshatch

Martha so admired, the "noble, selfsacrificing creature she was." She spent the spring of 1862 reading Elizabeth Gaskell's biography of the author, which she described to Sadie as "a sad history of sad lives":

> I think it is calculated, to make all petty trials insignificant, and lead the mind, to contemplate the heroic nobleness and admire the fortitude and courage which enabled those pure souls to remain unspotted or sink one step lower, ~~than~~ even though surrounded by vulgarity in its lowest type, ... wearisome, wearisome, must have been their lives, so chained and trampled down by relentless circumstances yet, their minds and souls so filled with ambitious aspiration and matchless intellectual power. Their examples of holy patience, and their constant faith and dependence upon the Father of all, impresses the mind with reverence. My heart often ached for poor dear Charlotte, who was so lonely and desolate, after her two dear loving almost idolized sister were called to their long home, how calmly, and nobly she submitted to Gods will, her faith and endurance and patience, may be a lessen and a comfort to many a distressed soul.[8]

Gaskell's biography was revolutionary in that it was one of the first to take women's personal lives seriously as objects of study. But in order to rehabilitate her friend and fellow author's reputation, Gaskell elided the more salacious details, sanding Brontë's life into an easily consumable morality tale. For Martha's sake, I wish it had been otherwise, leaving room for love and sex and anger at pain that *wasn't okay*, that *could not be endured*. Self-sacrifice was not something Martha needed to learn more about. But these were the narratives from which

8 MS to SB, Mar. 5, 1862.

young women constructed their futures.

* * *

In May 1859, toward the end of the school year, Martha's class held a party. After a gray morning, the sun came out, and Martha and her students prepared a throne for the May queen. Set in the middle of the Willets' orchard, the arch-backed dais sat atop a platform strewn with greenery and flowers. All of the girls carried bouquets and wore white. Martha wore white, too. She must have looked like one of them. They must have looked like a group of young brides without grooms: probably a safer, sweeter-seeming option to some of them. And whom could the throne have been for but Sadie, the sweetest and prettiest of a score of sweet and pretty girls, who was crowned queen and presided over the festivities? Later, neighbors joined the class for dinner. Tables sat among the trees, covered in flowers, cakes, ice cream, lemonade, strawberries, and other treats. The party delighted Martha, and why shouldn't it have? It was everything she loved about weddings, and none of what scared her about marriage.

After Martha and Sadie parted ways later that year, they wrote to each other about love. Sadie sometimes dreamed about a young man whose name she would not disclose. "if thee does not say who I will think it was nobody therefore thee may be an old maid," Martha teased. She was twenty, young enough that joking about old maids did not yet give her a twinge. She did not yet expect to be one.[9]

Sadie was pretty and blue-eyed, and many men pursued her. "Thy friend," Martha called one of Sadie's suitors, or "thy 'beau." A boy named Joe pursued Sadie so insistently that rumors swirled of their engagement. Sometimes suitors con-

9 MS to SB, Oct. 16, 1859.

spired with Martha to win Sadie's affections. "I did once write to thee for somebody else at his request!!!" Martha reminded her friend. Was it the same man who once ran off with Sadie's picture, which Martha had left on the table in her home?[10] When Martha's own picture disappeared from Sadie's house, Martha was glad. "I hope it is broken or rubbed out," she insisted, "no one would think it worth running away with." No one but her could want it.

Martha was, by her own description and in part by her own choice, a "school marm."[11] "How few [young men] there are that I would trust my happiness to," she wrote in her diary at age nineteen.[12] It was Valentine's Day of 1858, and she had neither sent nor expected to receive any valentines. Yet romance was not missing from her life: there was John Browne, "who acted like a perfect loof would try and kiss me and sit with his hand in my lap talked the greatest lot of nonsense all the time so I thought the time was wasted while he was here"; another John, who washed her face with snow after a sleigh ride; perhaps Edward Willets, the married man with whom she lodged while she taught at his school in Purchase, New York (though I don't believe this).[13] On Long Island, she flirted with a young man who lived near her aunt and uncle and often brought her the mail. He was "rather tall" though "not handsome," but he had "beautiful black eyes & very dark hair" (and "a slight moustache which I think horrid and have told him so.")[14] Oldden's cousin Ellis Ridgway, whom she liked but found immature, may have asked her to marry him.[15]

She could be a scamp when it came to romance, teasing

10 MS to SB, Mar. 16–17, 1862.
11 MS to SB, Apr. 15, July 3, 1860.
12 MS diary, Feb. 14, 1858.
13 MS diary, Jan. 3, 1858, Feb. 5, 1859.
14 MS to SB, March 11, 1860.
15 MS diary, Sept. 2, 1860.

her friends about their crushes and once even sending a fake valentine. "Thee spoke of Valentines," she wrote shortly after the holiday in 1860, "no yes I did send one." It was a joke; she had forgotten about it entirely. A group of children clamored for her to write one, and her aunt composed a poem to include. Martha sent the card to a man named William Titus, "a person I rather dislike."[16] No one was the wiser; Martha "was never suspected" and "the entire credit was given to another young lady whom I tease about him."[17] Hijinks aside, Martha's relationships with men, for various reasons, did not follow the same trajectory that Sadie's did.

* * *

"When Catherine is about seventeen," the protagonist's father, Dr. Sloper, thinks in Henry James's *Washington Square*, "[her aunt] Lavinia will try and persuade her that some young man with a moustache is in love with her. It will be quite untrue; no young man, with a moustache or without, will ever be in love with Catherine."[18]

James, or his narratorial stand-in, did not want to tell readers why this was so. "Her father, as he looked at her, often said to himself that, such as she was, he at least need have no fear. I say 'such as she was,' because, to tell the truth — But this is a truth of which I will defer the telling."[19]

Because the truth, the narrator reveals a few pages later, is that Catherine is not pretty. This, apparently, is what he (a pronoun I choose intentionally) could barely bring himself to tell us. "She was not ugly," he clarifies, "she had simply a plain, dull, gentle countenance. The most that had ever been

16 MS to SB, Mar. 11, 1860.

17 MS to SB, Mar. 11, 1860.

18 Henry James, *Washington Square* (1880; repr., New York: Penguin Books, 2003), 33–34.

19 James, *Washington Square*, 30.

Crosshatch

said for her was that she had a 'nice' face."[20]

Martha wasn't pretty either. In a picture from 1865, when she was twenty-six, her dark hair is short, tied back with a simple black ribbon, like Jo after she sells her hair ("her one beauty"). Her white dress is buttoned partway up her neck. The three-quarter profile and almost-smile soften her features, yet still I notice her thin lips and sharp jaw.

Martha rarely talked about her appearance. Her body, yes, but only because of her poor health. But being pretty did not seem to concern her. She sometimes recorded her weight, but it was because she wanted to weigh more, not less.

Martha could not vote, or go to college, or pursue most of the personal and professional opportunities that I take for granted. Yet she did not spend every day of her adolescence and young adulthood consumed by grief and anger at her ugliness. It sounds like incomprehensible freedom.

* * *

People in Martha and Sadie's lives were always getting married. Martha's friend Carrie Willets married in the fall of 1861. It was a small wedding, after which the couple left for Niagara, where they planned to spend the winter. *Don't become an old maid*, Carrie had once told Martha.

The next spring she attended her friend Lizzie Satterthwait's wedding. Lizzie wore a white silk dress and a wreath of blossoms in her dark hair. Her marble-pale skin made her look to Martha like a beautiful statue.

Her uncle Charley married. Her friend Eph married. Jacob A. married. There were two weddings on the same day in 1862. "Young folks will do it every where," Martha supposed.[21]

---

20 James, *Washington Square*, 34.
21 MS to SB, June 12, Nov. 2, 1862, Sept. 29, 1863, n.d. [ca. 1862, misla-

She did not mind the weddings. "I always like to hear of young folks getting married, for I think they will be happier, I do not mean, where it is merely for money, position, or the sake of being married, but where there is real true love."[22]

Friendships weren't the same once someone was married, though. "Dearly as I love my married friends," Martha confessed, "I find them poor correspondents, and I suppose I must not think they love me any the less only they have numerous duties to look after, and of course finding all they need of affection in their husbands, do not feel the necessity of expressing what they have for other friends." "Some how married people always seem different," agreed Sadie. What would happen when one or both of them married?[23]

Sometimes men wanted to marry Martha, but it was never for the right reasons. Some men were silly about marriage, wanting a wife for the sake of a wife, or likely for the sake of the labor she could provide. A Quaker and widower Martha knew was like that. "He is like some other widowers," she told Sadie, "foolish on the subject" of marriage. Martha found him disagreeable. This was not the life she wanted, but she had few choices: Friends discouraged marrying outside of the sect, though several of Martha's male friends did so.[24]

At some point, Martha realized that she – the spinster, the schoolmarm – would never marry. Even at twenty-four she felt it unlikely. "Thee need not prepare for my wedding till thee hears from me," she told Sadie. No matter how many other people got married, "one thing sartin I am safe yet, so thee need not calculate on my getting to my nuptial feast very soon." Sadie had forbidden Martha from marrying before she did, anyway. Anna had made Martha promise something

beled ca. 1857].

22 MS to SB, May 10, 1860.

23 MS to SB, Mar. 5, 1862; SB to MS, Oct. 7, 1863.

24 MS to SB, July 2, 1863.

Crosshatch

similar. All Martha could do was hope that she approved of Sadie's choice.[25]

Perhaps, Martha thought, it was for the best that she did not marry. So much could go wrong in marriage. Spouses could enter into it too lightly, or they could be mismatched, or they could be incapable of love at all. Spouses could die, especially during wartime. Children died, too. Once, in 1862, Martha went to visit a dying three-year-old child, burned beyond recovery in a barn fire. That same night, her beloved nephew Howard, Sallie's eldest child, burned his hands on the stove. As Martha tended to his blisters, she could not help thinking of the other child. Howard died of typhoid fever at just thirteen. Tragedies abounded. Better, perhaps, to avoid this heartbreak entirely.

---

25 MS to SB, Sept. 29, 1863.

CHAPTER SEVEN: HUSBAND

Martha did marry, though. In secret, away from the prying eyes of friends, relatives, and historians, Martha and Sadie wed. Perhaps it was in late 1863, when Martha visited Sadie in Brooklyn. Perhaps they were up late one night in Sadie's bedroom, the rest of her family fast asleep. Early that year, Martha had given Sadie a ring she had received from a soldier. "He will not care," she figured, "& thee can wear it for my sake." Perhaps, if Martha woke before Sadie, her eyes would alight on the ring on her best friend's hand. From then on, Sadie was Martha's wife, and Martha was Sadie's husband.[1]

Not from then on, actually. But for a while.

When the school year ended in 1859, Martha and Sadie vacationed together at Chappaqua, a Quaker-founded village along the Hudson River. In July 1861 – the next time they saw each other – Martha visited Sadie in Brooklyn. They walked in the orchard behind Sadie's home and saw the sights: Trinity Church and Central Park, not yet complete. When Martha returned home, she sat alone in her quiet bedroom, listening to crickets chirp outside and trying not to cry.

Sadie's parents finally brought her to Darby in July 1862. They visited Independence Hall and the Woodlands, shared

1 MS to SB, Mar. 1, 1863.

ice cream and lemonade and moonlit walks with Martha's friends. Alone, they gathered moss and fern along the creek, a cool trickle of reprieve at the peak of the sweltering mid-Atlantic summer. One long, hot afternoon, Martha read to Sadie until Sadie fell asleep. One wonders if they wish to unencumber themselves of their heavy garments. Even the nightgowns they wore as they slept next to each other were long-sleeved, high-necked, floor-length. But they were loose, and far less layered.

When it was time to leave, she and Martha went into Philadelphia, then across the river to Camden, New Jersey. Martha waited as Sadie's train pulled away. "With an effort I kept back the burning tears," Martha confessed. It felt as if a light had been snuffed out. The two were already so close that they hoped to die together.[2]

Somewhere, Martha's missing diary – the one that covers from February 1863 until June 1864 – details her reactions to events that took place in both the nation and her personal life in these months, when her relationship with Sadie deepened into a marriage in its own right. It seems more than a coincidence that this diary, the one I most want to see, is not extant.

Something must have happened in January 1864, when Martha visited Sadie in Brooklyn. After this trip, they began referring to each other as "husband" and "wife." "Good night my own dear wife," Martha closed the letter she began writing on the train ride home, as soon as she stopped crying. Once, she accidentally (so she claimed) addressed a letter to "Sadie M. Schofield," giving Sadie her own last name.[3]

Sadie thought about Martha in the bath; she thought about her in bed. "Tonight I am tired," she once wrote, "<u>have taken a bath</u> which makes me feel better, I am not very sleepy, will think of thee in bed," remembering when they were

2 MS diary, July 26, 1862.
3 MS to SB, Apr. 2, 1865.

together. "Would thee like to know how thy <u>wife looked</u>, she asked another time, after a sociable. "Imagine her in a dress of plain white swiss with blue sash trimmed at the ends with silver fringe, white kid gloves and slippers, hair rolled in front and a water-fall back <u>decorated</u> with pink buds and white clematis." That night she lay alone in her room, "thinking of my husband away off in Darby."[4]

Only once did Sadie suggest it was a game, calling herself "thy loving 'wife,'" with the last word in quotation marks. She didn't usually do this. Did Martha, the school marm, notice this subtle difference?[5]

* * *

Women's nineteenth-century friendships often looked more like what we today think of as romantic relationships. More than forty years ago, historian Carroll Smith-Rosenberg wrote the famous article "The Female World of Love and Ritual: Relations between Women in Nineteenth-Century America," which explained women's intimate friendships within their social and cultural context rather than, as previous historians had done, individual psychology or sexuality. Women friends loved each other passionately. They addressed each other as lovers and yearned to hug and kiss each other. "An undeniably romantic and even sensual note frequently marked female friendships," Smith-Rosenberg wrote.[6]

These attachments were perfectly acceptable within white, middle-class society, which separated women and men from each other physically and emotionally. According to Smith-Rosenberg, "female friendships were frequently sup-

---

4 SB to MS, Jan. 21, 1864, Mar. 21, 1865.
5 SB to MS, Mar. 21, 1865.
6 Carroll Smith-Rosenberg, "The Female World of Love and Ritual: Relations between Women in Nineteenth-Century America," *Signs* 1 (1975): 24.

ported and paralleled by severe social restrictions on intimacy between young men and women." Women developed their own emotional world, of which devotion to one another was a part. Most of them married men, though marriage did not displace their female friendships.[7]

In the decades since, queer historians have taken Smith-Rosenberg to task for refusing to see these relationships as sexual. Surely many of them were. Desire is powerful, and how easily a hand could stray, lips could graze flesh, minds knowing only that the closeness felt right. Why not, if nothing taught against it? Nothing did, not really. That's one of the beautiful aspects of history: in the interstices of even the most repressive culture – in this case, one that otherwise denied women agency over their sexuality – lie pockets where people can create joy. Why not act on these instincts, then? If Martha had sex with anyone, it was probably Sadie. Logistics alone make other possibilities unlikely.

* * *

In Darby in 1862, Sadie met Martha's friend Thomas Chalkley (Chalk) Bartram. Sadie thought she made a bad first impression on Chalk, too excited and overly familiar. He "must have thought me a wild 'Yank Gal,'" she remembered.[8] Afterwards he sometimes imagined that he saw Sadie. "Chalk says he thought he saw thee on Chestnut St. the other day," Martha relayed.[9] Or he tried to take from Martha the letters Sadie had written to her. "Chalk was in the Office" one day when Martha stopped by to pick up Sadie's message "& quite anxious to read it himself – ; which I did not choose then."[10]

---

7 Smith-Rosenberg, "The Female World of Love and Ritual," 9.
8 SB to MS, Apr. 9, 1865.
9 MS to SB, Nov. 29, 1862.
10 MS to SB, June 8, 1863.

Crosshatch

Still, it was a surprise when six year later, in 1868, Chalk proposed to Sadie, and she said yes. Martha cut out big chunks of her diary that year and the next, when Sadie and Chalk married. "Destroy all this <u>unread</u>!" she wrote in where 1869 begins.

It was not that Martha mistrusted Chalk, one of her oldest and dearest friends. When the two had merely been courting, she felt nothing but happiness for them. But marriage – this was a different beast entirely. "In my intense joy at her happiness," Martha confessed to her diary upon learning of the engagement, "I did not at first realize my own bitter grief – . But now, now that she tells me she is a 'promised wife,' there comes into my heart a crushing weight, a burden heavy to be borne – … The bitterness the agony, that comes with the consciousness of her needing <u>me</u> <u>less</u>, of her turning from me, to find peace, comfort, rest, on another's love."[11]

For over a decade, Martha had coiled her love ever tighter around Sadie's heart, thinking no one else could ever gain access. Perhaps she had been foolish to think so. After all, it had happened before. "All these I have loved & who loved me," she wrote, "have found others dearer still, one by one they have left me standing alone." But her love for Sadie, and Sadie's love for her, were different, weren't they? Surely they would cling together always. "I know that no future lover can drive from thy mind the image of <u>thy first</u> husband," Martha had written to Sadie in 1864. Sadie was "my last, and dearest, my most precious and cherished, my idol, my darling." Must even Martha's "little 'ewe lamb'" be "given into another's keeping"?[12]

Martha, meanwhile, stood alone.

"My own life never looked so hopeless, cheerless, desolate as it does now," she wrote some two weeks later, "indeed I

---

11 MS diary, Jan. 2, 1869.
12 MS diary, Jan. 2, 1869; MS to SB, May 1, 1864.

have <u>no</u> hope for the future – only to die – ."[13]

Back in Darby, Martha's sister Eliza watched Chalk with curiosity. Was he worthy of her sister's dearest friend, to whom she had also grown close? Perhaps not. But Sadie may make him worthy. Perhaps she could convince him to quit smoking. Perhaps, for her, he would do so willingly. "He has many, many noble qualities," Sadie insisted. Eliza hoped he would be a good husband.[14]

Two years younger than Martha, Eliza never married. Neither did Lydia, the twin of Martha's married sister, Sallie. Both knew how Martha must be feeling. "One after another of my friends have either married or died," Eliza wrote. What was the difference, really? Women followed their spouses as a matter of course, sometimes so far away that it seemed to their friends at home as if they were dead. That was how Eliza felt when her last remaining friend married. "She too has gone, and <u>so</u> <u>far</u> <u>away</u> that it seems like never having her anymore." It was all well and good for Sallie, "our <u>happy</u> Sister," to say, as she did, that Martha, Eliza, and Lydia should "'go & do likewise' link our hearts by an inseparable tie to some manly heart." Even if it were that easy, no manly heart could compensate for the disappearance of a beloved.[15]

Sadie promised Martha that they would remain as close as ever. "Do not think because he has claimed thy Sadie to be nearer than a friend – that thy helping heart must withdraw its influence … Friendship is too sacred to <u>ever change</u>."[16] But of course it would.

* * *

13 Pencil marks in margin, MS diary, between Dec. 31, 1868, and Jan. 1, 1869; MS diary, Jan. 19, 1869.
14 Eliza Schofield to MS, Mar. 29, 1869; SB to MS, July 2, 1869.
15 Eliza Schofield to MS, Mar. 29, 1869; Lydia Schofield to MS, Mar. 28, 1869.
16 SB to MS, July 2, 1869.

Crosshatch

Sadie and Chalk wed in October 1869. Martha spent two weeks in Brooklyn tending to preparations with her beloved, all the while hoping that Sadie could not read her deepest thoughts. "Every hour the <u>pain</u> comes to <u>me</u>, that I am loosing my own darling," she wrote. Sadie mustn't know the loneliness and desolation Martha felt as they sat in Sadie's room and sewed, as they baked her wedding cake together. Sadie was nervous these days, excitable, especially when Martha's sadness became obvious.[17] Did the pain show up in crooked stitches, lumpy batter? But if Martha's eyes were red, she could blame hours spent staring at her needle; a pale face could be an errant dusting of flour. Women's work could distract from women's pain.

Martha and Sadie spent the night before the wedding holding each other. The bridal shower that evening was lovely. Martha had arranged the flowers beautifully, and Sadie's other friends overwhelmed her with gifts. The bride-to-be stayed up after her guests had gone to bed, but Martha retired to Sadie's bedroom. Lying awake, she "realized the bond that bound her to another & made her less my own." Sadie came to join her, and they lay in each other's arms until morning.[18] Martha must have hoped that the sun would never rise, or that, when it did, the new day would offer possibilities that the previous one had not. But Martha would have had to wait a century, not a night, to live the life she may have wanted.

There was still much to do the next morning, but Martha couldn't bear to be around others for long. Preparing the house for the festivities, she snuck off two or three times to weep alone. "I longed to get away and be alone with my pain," she wrote. But she could not, and so she tried to forget herself entirely. Sadie was going to be happy. She must focus

---

17 MS diary, Sept. 30. Oct. 1, 9, 6, 1869.
18 MS diary, Oct. 12, 1869.

on that alone.[19]

The ceremony was in the parlor, a little before one o'clock in the afternoon. Sixty guests filled the room, but it was quiet, a "solemn silence" overlaid with "the stillness of death." Strange words to describe a wedding. Perhaps prophetic. Sadie, Chalk, and their closest friends stood in silence for several minutes in front of the guests. Chalk removed his glove, and the ceremony began. He and Sadie exchanged simple gold bands and said their vows. Martha had never heard Sadie speak with such gravitas, such feeling, as when her beloved promised to be Chalk's wife.[20]

The exchange lasted just a few minutes, no longer than the silence that preceded the ceremony. But for Martha it was agony. "It seemed as if all I had, my very life — was going away from me," she wrote. Tears trickled down her cheeks as she trembled. Her heart felt like it was bursting. She meant this literally: she feared she would hemorrhage.[21]

"Seek ye first the kingdom of heaven, and all things else will be added unto you." The words from Matthew 6:33 bore a special meaning for Friends, Martha among them. Worldly desires were not the point. It was the same advice John had given Martha when he instructed her to find a better life. When her friend Esther Haviland spoke these words to Martha after the wedding, it calmed her. She had lost Sadie, but she could do without. She would be fine, or so she claimed. After all, the art of losing isn't hard to master. Martha enjoyed the food and the flowers and, finally, the ferry back to Philadelphia.[22]

Sadie and Chalk traveled to their new home apart from the rest of the guests that night. Martha visited them after breakfast the next morning. Sadie led Martha to her room,

19 MS diary, Oct. 13, 1869.
20 MS diary, Oct. 13, 1869.
21 MS diary, Oct. 13, 1869.
22 MS diary, Oct. 13, 1869.

Crosshatch

and the two were alone for the first time since the wedding. "She is my own still," Martha wrote, "those few minutes are burned into my brain never to be iffaced."[23] What must have happened in those few minutes? An embrace, a stolen kiss, a promise? Surely no more, with time so short and Chalk downstairs.

Martha stayed in Darby through the end of October. It was painful for her to leave, especially with Sadie now close by. "My attractions here are stronger than ever," she wrote. She hid this pain perhaps too well. "Ah — ! they — all think I don't feel these partings." But she could not leave her work, the better life that lay beyond the material world.[24]

Staying in Darby presented its own challenges, anyway, as dinner with John and Anna turned to supper with Sadie and Chalk, all of her married friends whose unions she had helped to facilitate. *Some how married people always seem different,* Sadie had observed years earlier. Now she was the one who had changed.[25]

* * *

Sadie was happy as Chalk's wife. They had a son, Frank, born in 1871, and a daughter, Mary, born in 1875. Shortly after the wedding, Sadie wondered to Martha how long her time as a wife would last.[26] She was twenty-five then, not so very young. But she could not have predicted that it would be less than nine years.

She had been sick for some time when she died at eleven in the evening on May 19, 1878, from heart trouble exacerbated by a recent trip to New York. Martha didn't know until

---

23 MS diary, Oct. 14, 1869.
24 MS diary, Oct. 16, 31, 1869.
25 MS diary, Oct. 31, 1869.
26 SB to MS, Nov. 3, 1869.

a letter from Sadie's aunt Sarah reached her several days later, and there was no time to travel to Darby for the funeral on the twenty-second. If only Sadie and Chalk had hired a nurse, as Aunt Sarah had repeatedly asked them to do, though of course it might not have made any difference. Sadie was only thirty-four.[27]

In the early afternoon, the Bartrams' house filled with mourners. Sadie wore a black silk dress, a gift from her aunt Sarah, which she had worn for the first time at a wedding the night before she got sick. (It would have looked better without the overskirt, Martha's sister Lydia thought.) Martha's sister Sallie had begged Chalk to save a part of the sash for his daughter, Mary, but he refused. Sallie cut out a part of the back of the dress instead. Sadie's hair and the top part of her face looked pretty, but below that she was swollen. Lydia sat beside Sadie in the parlor, kissing her on the forehead for both Martha and herself. Someone, likely Chalk, took off Sadie's wedding ring just before they nailed the lid onto the coffin. His face was very pale.[28]

At the grave, Martha's brother-in-law, Samuel Ash, read a telegram from Martha to Chalk. "I mourn with you," it began. Martha had introduced Sadie to Darby, Samuel reminded the mourners. He and Chalk murmured a few more words to each other, but their voices were too low for anyone to hear.

The gravesite was a lovely spot in the cemetery, under a large tree. The foliage compensated for the fact that Chalk had forbidden flowers. They must have seemed incongruous with his grief.[29]

Martha volunteered to pay for a headstone for Sadie, and in June she and Chalk made plans to pick one out. Both

27 S[arah] J. Mott to MS, May 19, 1878; Lydia Schofield to MS, May 23, 1878.
28 Lydia Schofield to MS, May 23, 1878.
29 Lydia Schofield to MS, May 23, 1878.

Crosshatch

hoped that it would be white and pretty. Martha's generosity surprised Chalk; he promised to maintain discretion.[30] It was an unconventional offer.

Frank and Mary were eight and three when Sadie died. They bore it well, though it was hard for Chalk to buy clothes for Mary. Female relatives, including Sadie's mother, who stayed in Darby for a while after her daughter's death, helped him take care of her. Shortly after Sadie's death, Martha offered to take Mary in herself. But Chalk didn't need help for long, as it turned out. Three years later, he remarried. Chalk outlived his second wife, Anna Wollaston, too. But their marriage lasted longer than Chalk and Sadie's. [31]

At some point after Sadie's death, Chalk must have found the letters Martha wrote to his wife and returned them to their author. There is no other way to explain the letters' presence in Martha's papers. One wonders at the scene. One wonders if he read them, and, if so, how he felt about Sadie's longest and most important relationship.

* * *

Martha visited Sadie one last time before leaving for the South in 1865. On July 18 they dressed up and had their pictures taken. Sadie wore a white dress, and Martha borrowed a dark brown one. They were the same size. "I am so pleased with us," Martha wrote. She and her daughter or twin or wife had been immortalized together. "Thee my other self," Sadie once called Martha. In the picture Sadie's hair is down, so long it almost touches the floor. In 1914 Martha gave the picture to Frank, who never married or had any children. Neither did Mary. The picture is unlikely to resurface.[32]

---

30 T. Chalkley Bartram to MS, June 25, 1878.
31 T. Chalkley Bartram to MS, May 25, 1879.
32 SB to MS, July 2, 1869; MS diary, July 18, 1865.

But buried in my folder of college writing, I find an image that reminds me of Martha and Sadie, perhaps along the Hudson River at Chappaqua. It's a postcard of the painting "Summer Evening on the Southern Beach," by the Norwegian painter Peter Severin Kröyer (1851–1900). In it, two women in nearly identical white dresses walk down a deserted beach, arms linked, heads turned toward each other. In the background, the grays of the sky, sea, and sand blur into one another. At some points, the three are nearly indistinguishable, as are the two women. The one wearing a hat is slightly taller. Her hair may be slightly lighter, or it may just be the way the evening light hits it. The other, slightly shorter, holds her hat in her hand. They could be sisters or lovers. Their faces might help us distinguish between them, but they face away from the viewer, only the hint of profile visible on one of them. Like Martha and Sadie, they will keep their secrets.

Interlude: Lives of Girls and Women

"What is sex?" my best friend, Ashley, asked me one day when I was twelve and she was eleven. "Is it just when people take their clothes off and look at each other, or is it something more than that?" Ashley smushed naked Barbie and Ken dolls together just fine, but I guess she didn't make the connection. I haven't found any pictures of Sadie, so I picture her as Ashley, who was small and blonde and had lots of boyfriends, who surely learned from experience what sex was long before I did. It made me burn with jealousy.

I blushed. "I ... think it's something more than that."

I knew, but barely. Health class at my conservative private school didn't include sex ed. We separated for health class, where the girls' gym teacher taught us about puberty and periods and I guess probably also penises a little bit, at least their role in the reproductive system. But mostly I remember learning about periods. With the teacher's encouragement, we told the boys it was a baking class.

Did the boys ever tell us anything about what they were learning? I don't think so, but it was enough to make them all laugh when Jake pointed out a stain on the back of my pants. Maybe they didn't care what we thought. Maybe they didn't think their bodies were anything to be ashamed of. Maybe they just never felt like they owed us anything the way we felt like we owed them.

* * *

By the time I was aware of romance novels, Fabio was already a joke, just the cheesy guy in the "I Can't Believe It's Not Butter" commercials whom I sometimes confused with Michael Bolton or Kenny G. It's hard to keep track. There were a lot of longhaired, B-list, cheeseball celebrities in the early 1990s.

But home sick from school one day in 1994, I snuck Judith McNaught's *Until You* from my mother's bookshelf, and this, dear reader, is how I once and for all learned what sex was. I hid this and similar books under my mattress, where I never felt them. I'm not a real princess, you see.

There's not nearly enough sex in *Until You*, and the scenes that are there aren't even that good. They're gross and rapey, and the hero is always taking the heroine's breasts out of her dress the way you would choose a blueberry muffin from a Dunkin' Donuts bag. They're also where I finally learned the mechanics of intercourse, and if I were to answer Ashley's question, it was the knowledge I had to draw on.

The most important lesson these books have to teach, though, isn't about sex at all. It's about patriarchy: the heroine is always blamed for something she doesn't know she did or something she didn't even do. In *Until You*, Sheridan Bromleigh, a twenty-year-old American teacher, has been hired to accompany one of her students to London. Through a series of misadventures, Sheridan loses her memory and comes to believe she is engaged to Stephen Westmoreland, the handsome, wealthy Earl of Langford. The two fall in love, but when Sheridan regains her memory, Stephen assumes she has been conning him all along. They reunite, of course, and the novel tries to absolve Stephen for his abuse. Rich and titled, he is accustomed to women pursuing him only for his money and position. How can anyone blame Stephen for thinking Sheridan is lying, just like all other women?

These are the Rules of Romance Novels: there's always an explanation for *why men are the way they are*. Decades ago, feminist theorist Janice Radway identified this pattern as the utopian element of romance novels: they allow readers to simultaneously protest against and come to terms with patriarchy. Their narrative structure brings a sense of order and logic to it; it explains the puzzling or upsetting behavior of the men in readers' own lives.

The relationship between romance novels and their readers is, of course, much, much more complicated than that. Of course, they can be sources of genuine, liberatory pleasure. But this reader, at least, was more than happy to internalize the message Radway identifies.

I spent much of 1997 and 1998 working on "Aurora's Harbinger," a dystopian screenplay set ten to fifteen years in the future. It's a pretty classic story: society has been taken over – or reformed, depending on one's point of view – by a group that believes humanity has been so corrupted by technology that its only hope is to start over, to live as the early European settlers in North America lived. The relationship between Mira, the protagonist, and Stephen, her love interest, is pure Radway. Stephen is alternately warm and kind and cold and cruel to Mira. At one point, he asks her if she is an angel. Later he kisses her, but only because he "had no choice. It was either that or slap you. You were hysterical." Over the course of a few dozen pages, he professes and promptly rescinds his love on about three hundred separate occasions.

Surely I did not *want* this kind of a relationship. Did I?

Once, waiting for Ashley to come downstairs from the attic, I peeked at her mother's diary, which lay in the empty computer room.

"The person who should be my best friend is the one who terrifies me most," it read. Ashley's dad left shortly thereafter. That's what marriage could really be like. This was the stolen lesson about heteronormative, patriarchal romance I should have heeded, rather than those I found in softcore lady porn.

* * *

For one brief period in my late teens and early twenties, I imagined a normal life for myself: marriage, motherhood, all of the accoutrements of adult femininity I've otherwise never desired. At the very same time, I began to learn about and eventually fall in love with feminism.

I was in college, miserable and lonely and unsure of myself, and probably more shaken by world events than I realized – or perhaps I just say this now to justify how desperately I wanted to be taken care of. I knew a conventional life wasn't for me (I wanted so much more than that, after all), but I also couldn't imagine another. I didn't have the same gumption Martha had to envision and create a kind of life that had never been lived before. There I was, nearly 150 years later, incapable or not brave enough to pursue what by then was a well-trod feminist path.

By day, I learned terms like "hegemonic masculinity" and "gender performativity." By night, I fantasized about taking my children to the playground at Washington Square Park, the other moms judging me because they knew I was a weirdo. I even fantasized about baby names (yes, dear reader, one of them was Aiden).

The men I longed for were conventional too – tennis player Andy Roddick, my studio classmate Rob, who in looks and mannerisms bore an uncanny resemblance to the (very) young Warren Beatty of *Splendor in the Grass*.

Late at night, after performances, Rob and I got drunk

Crosshatch

on sake or in the dark back rooms of wine bars along with a small group of fellow actors. It sounds deliciously grown-up and literary, a midcentury short story come to life, and it was, all of my Dorothy Parker fantasies come true. Cold War–like existential fears in the air, too: when would the (next) attack come? Heidi and I sat at the table and gossiped while the men went to the counter to order drinks for us, and it felt for once like I was a woman.

One night, after several glasses of wine, I ignored the voice from my introduction to women's studies class and proclaimed to Rob, "I guess I'm just conservative when it comes to gender."

What? I knew that this was no longer true. But he was conservative when it came to gender too, he told me, and perhaps I thought that saying so would finally make him like me.

* * *

When such narratives presented themselves, of course, the reality was very different. When a young man approached me in Penn Station in the fall of 2000, I didn't know what to do. He was a few years older than me, handsome, with a Russian accent. It was my first year in college, and I was waiting for my train home for Thanksgiving break. It was early in the morning, at least for a college student, and I was already regretting not taking a shower. Though it was November, I had still managed to get sweaty on my way to the train station. As the drops rolled down my face, they exacerbated the irritation from my acne medication, the sting was so painful it brought tears to my eyes and bleached all of my clothes yet somehow did nothing for the painful cysts on my cheeks. I always remembered that line from a Judy Blume book, about painful cysts on a girl's cheeks. It wasn't a main character. It was a main character's sister, and who wants to be that? But that's who you are when your cheeks are covered in acne, when the waistline of your pants digs into your stomach, soft and bulgy from too many late-night pizza slices, eaten after too many cranberries and vodka, consumed on an empty stomach, because then you could get drunk more quickly and on fewer calories.

He sat down next to me, a bit closer than I was comfortable with. "Please leave me alone," I could have said, but I didn't. I didn't think I had that right. We talked for a little while, or he talked to me. He asked for my phone number, which I stupidly gave him. Eventually he kissed me, and I let him. What didn't I know I was allowed to say no?

Eventually he started asking about the ring I was wearing. It was my high school class ring, which I wore out of habit rather than any sort of loyalty. I should give it to him, he said, and he would give it back to me the next time he saw me. I refused. He kept asking. Finally my train was called, and I joined the horde walking down the steps to the platform.

In the weeks to come, he called me several times. On the phone, he pressed to see me. He told me that he loved me. My roommates thought this was weird and creepy, and eventually I stopped answering.

Only gradually, and only much later, did I realize that I was a mark. I'm sure of it. It was this young man's job to seduce naïve young girls — unpretty young girls, girls who would be grateful for any crumbs of male attention — into giving him their valuables, at which point he would disappear. Had I given him my ring, I never would have heard from him again. He would have pawned it, I suppose, or given it to his boss.

* * *

Alex was different. We became friends the summer after high school graduation, awkwardly ambling down Main Street as

Crosshatch

we discussed our dreams for the future and my Keds rubbed my ankles raw. Alex was assigned male at birth and presented this way for most of our relationship, but at her request I use her correct pronouns throughout this text. She was in love with me, she told me some months later. I didn't reciprocate, and on some level I knew I was in no shape to be someone's girlfriend. But by the fall of 2002 I was deranged with loneliness.

In the end, it was a simple equation: an ex-goth punk, a theater nerd, two bottles of wine, and an empty dorm room.

I had never been in a relationship before. I had kissed lots of my theater friends playing truth or dare in the hot tub, and two years earlier I had drunkenly made out with my roommate's friend from home. I didn't especially like him, but his leather jacket felt nice, smooth and cool to the touch after too many cranberry and vodkas at the bar that ignored my pigtails and all of our obviously fake IDs. I had no interest in seeing him again. Some weeks later, during the Florida recount, he left rude, pro-Bush comments on my AIM away messages.

Bush was a bully. This boy was a bully. Everywhere there were macho bullies. I was scared of them and, truth be told, all men: the power they had to define, to devalue. To destroy. Part of what I liked about Alex was that she wasn't like that. She was sensitive and wore eyeliner and wrote poetry, more Robert Smith than George W. Bush. Rainer Maria Rilke in her messenger bag, vegan Doc Martens on her feet, post-punk emo bands on her résumé.

Jo to Marmee in the 2019 *Little Women*, after she turns down Laurie's proposal: I care more to be loved. I want to be loved.

Marmee to Jo: That is not the same thing as loving.

My own Marmee could have told me something similar, had I given her the opportunity. I'm sure I wouldn't have listened, though. I *refuse* to listen to what anyone tells me. I *insist* on making my own mistakes. That's why I had student loans into my forties. Yet as I plunged my life into disaster after disaster, it never occurred to me that I could say, *No, thank you.* I'm as stubborn as Jo but with nowhere near her self-respect.

There were good times and bad in our relationship. I graduated from college, moved home, started grad school, finished grad school, adjuncted until I could stand it no longer, quit, and eventually found a job that I love. We moved together to Washington, DC, in 2005 and home(ish) to Philadelphia in 2015, the year that both the country and our relationship really started to fall apart.

* * *

Here is what I learned as a baby feminist twenty years ago:

Sex is biological; gender is social and cultural. Or perhaps sex too was a construction created by gender, if your reading of Judith Butler went beyond *Gender Trouble.* Either way, gender didn't have a biological basis, which is not the same as saying it isn't real.

Sex is biological; gender is social and cultural. It became a litany of sorts at the beginning of every women's studies class, a call-and-response between teacher and student that went on long enough for me to play both roles.

I learned that sexuality, too, has a history, one in which love and desire predate the contemporary social categories into which we organize our identities, categories that cannot then be read back on the past.

Finally, I was trained to think that unknowability – the inability to label something or figure out exactly what it was – was a radical and destabilizing phenomenon, for there *was* no ultimate truth.

By my mid-thirties, I started to realize that my cultural

Crosshatch

politics were hopelessly out of date, as the naming of identities became more and more important. Students pushed me: why couldn't I just *say*, for example, that a historical figure was a lesbian? Claiming an identity is, of course, a way of claiming visibility and legitimacy. I admit, though, that it can sometimes seem strange to me, someone trained to think that the refusal to be categorized was the radical act. I don't think either of these perspectives is necessarily better than the other. It's just a point of inflection that separates me from younger Millennials and our generational successors.

I'd like to think that this early training explains why I've never been particularly interested in ferreting out what Martha "really was." I'm comfortable with an ambiguous queerness, one that resists categorization. Less generously, I don't *need* Martha to have been a lesbian to see myself in history. As a straight (white, cisgender, middle-class, able-bodied) woman, I see myself everywhere.

I'll probably never abandon social constructivism as the main way I understand the world. I'll probably never believe in stable, transhistorical identities that exist across time and place. Ironically or appropriately, this academic skepticism is too deeply ingrained in how I think about myself and myself-in-the-world. These ideas are written onto my body, into my neural pathways, where they ultimately blur the lines between the social and biological, which is how it should be. I am a primary document.

* * *

Despite how much I identify with Martha, I sympathize with Sadie too, with the choices she made. Perhaps I should be angry with her for leaving Martha, for not being strong enough to think her way out of the social conventions of her time. Sometimes I am.

But I also know this: I am the Sadie of my story, or of someone else's story, really. I should not be writing this. Sadie should not write Martha's story. I am the one who said, I love you, but not enough. Not enough to ignore my own desires, or lack thereof.

"What if I wore a dress to our wedding?" Alex asked me several times in the spring of 2015, the same spring I realized how old and out of touch I was. I was unemployed and needed health insurance.

"That ... seems like an awful lot of trouble to go to for something that doesn't matter," I replied. I was showing my disdain by caring as little as possible, down to wearing gym clothes to the ceremony. I didn't understand why anyone would want to put in more effort than that. For me, femininity had only been restrictive, not liberating.

I realize now, of course, that this was a shitty thing to say. Alex and I had never really talked about trans identities except generally, theoretically, as something we obviously supported as part of our general lefty politics. Our relationship began, after all, with a screening of *Hedwig and the Angry Inch*. But in real life, it just wasn't what I wanted.

So, we broke up. It was for many reasons, but mostly it was because of gender, because of sexuality, because of what I couldn't feel.

I wondered about my own attractions. Was I attracted to some people and not others because of how I was positioned in history or because of *who I was*, and could these characteristics be separated, and did it matter? Was I too allowed to want, or not want, even if that wanting was a construction, an accident of history, of where I was located in time and place?

Sometimes, most of the time, I felt no desire. Sometimes, most of the time, I just felt numb. On the rare occasions that I did feel something, it was for the Olympic men's swim team, 1996–present (yes, even Ryan Lochte, please forgive me), feel-

Crosshatch

ings left over, no doubt, from being a girl swimmer, sucking in my stomach and staring at the boys on Saturday mornings and Wednesday evenings all summer long.

These feelings bothered me. I did not want to be, or to be found, on the wrong side of history. I did not want to be judged or pitied for not being able to escape my repressive cultural training. "She was a product of her time," future historians might say, shaking their heads ruefully.

"You're not going to be one of those terrible wives I read about on message boards who insists they're really straight, are you?" Alex asked me once. That was exactly what I was. Was it really so terrible? I didn't think so, not really. But most good and modern people seem to agree that leaving your trans partner makes you a villain.

I was thirty-seven years old and didn't know whom or what I wanted, or I did but felt I wasn't allowed to express it. Perhaps I was too old for all of this, but then Simone de Beauvoir was thirty-nine when she met Nelson Algren. I tested myself, trying to remember how and what I learned about what sex and romance were supposed to be, seeing if it made me feel anything. Call it the Jamie Fraser test (or, I suppose, the Sam Heughan test, since I've never actually read *Outlander*, only watched the television show).

Maybe I should read *Outlander*.

(Diana Gabaldon has a PhD, after all.)

I spent seminars fantasizing about the married, ten-years-younger-than-I-am, totally-awkward-but-kinda-looked-like-Mark-Ruffalo-if-you-squint grad student sitting beside me. He always addressed me as doctor no matter how many emails I signed with my first name. I found myself flirting – with Lyft drivers, with my tennis instructor – just to see what it felt like. It felt strange to have become that: a middle-aged divorcée, flirting with her significantly younger tennis instructor to feel better about herself, carefully shaving her legs and covering up her adult acne before each lesson.

(For the record, he flirted with me first, finding ways to touch me even when he wasn't correcting my forehand grip. But he probably didn't know that I imagined climbing onto his lap on the couch, trying not to spill my glass of wine while leaning in to kiss him.)

I still didn't know exactly what I wanted. But I had started to wake up.

CHAPTER EIGHT: TEACHER

In 1903, W. E. B. DuBois opined on "the crusade of the New England school-ma'am": "Behind the mists of ruin and rapine waved the calico dresses of women who dared. Rich and poor they were, serious and curious. Bereaved now of a father, now of a brother, now of more than these, they came seeking a life work in planting New England schoolhouses among the white and black of the South." Others were not so kind to the Northern white women who moved South to teach freed people after the Civil War. Southern white journalist Wilber J. Cash called them "horsefaced, bespectacled, and spare of frame." Martha learned in 1866 that an aide to General James B. Steedman, who had been sent South by President Johnson in 1866 to investigate Freedmen's Bureau activities and whom Martha found relatively sympathetic, had told some of her neighbors that "the teachers from the North were the scum of society – of doubtful reputation &c – he heard we were going to make it a permanent home & they might to make it to hot for us &c – ." Clearly these men found their presence threatening.[1]

By the 1860s, Northern white women were a force to be

---

1 W. E. B. DuBois, *The Souls of Black Folks* (Chicago: A. C. McClurg & Co., 1903), 64, 65; Wilbur J. Cash, *The Mind of the South* (New York: Knopf, 1941), 141; MS diary, May 24, 1866.

reckoned with. They were increasingly well-educated, and technological and market developments meant that their labor was less necessary at home. More – like Martha and two of her three sisters – remained single, and those who did marry, like her sister Sallie, did so later. But what were these women, so desperate to be useful, to do with themselves? Their professional opportunities had not kept pace with their educational ones. They could not all be teachers. Many of them did not want to be. But many of them, by choice, necessity, calling, or a combination thereof, did pursue this path, one of few respectable forms of paid labor open to women. For many of them, this path led South, where there was a desperate need for teachers in schools for newly freed Black people.

In truth, Northern white women like Martha made up less than half of the teachers in Southern Black schools after the Civil War. One third of the teachers were Black women from both North and South, and another quarter were Southern white women. Not all were young; not all were abolitionists; not all were middle-class; not all were women.

Not all were sojourners. Martha, in many ways, representative of the popular image of this group: young, educated, single, middle-class, from an abolitionist stronghold. She differed from the vast majority of her cohort in at least one significant way, however: she dedicated the rest of her life to the endeavor. In 1865–66, the first year she lived in South Carolina, she was one of 1,293 Northern white teachers in Southern Black schools. By 1876, that number had dwindled to 230, a group among which Quakers loomed large.

* * *

When Martha wrote to abolitionist James Miller McKim of the Port Royal Relief Association in February 1863, she had known for some time that it was her "duty to become a

Crosshatch

teacher among the poor degraded, but now free people of the South." Port Royal Island, off the coast of South Carolina, had been in Union hands since 1862; in January of that year, Phil Price, the brother of Martha's uncle Paxson Price, had come by the house looking for recruits to aid in relief efforts.[2]

Challenges abounded for Martha, starting with money: she lacked the funds to travel south and provide for herself once there. There was her health, which had always limited her ability to teach in the North, though she hoped a warm climate would suit her better. Then there were the ties of home and family. Martha was willing to give these up, but she anticipated opposition from her family, especially her mother – selfish, Martha thought, when so many families were giving up sons to the war.

McKim's response must have disappointed her, though she allowed that it was "gentlemanly": his committee was not funding any teachers at the moment, and he knew of no other agencies that were. For six months she nursed her disappointment alone, "bearing in my own mind the burden of that unfulfilled duty."[3]

Then she wrote to William Lloyd Garrison, who never responded.

Then she wrote to Oliver Johnson in the New York office of the American Anti-Slavery Society, pouring out her soul. "The spirit within me will not rest," she told him, "while there is so much need of work." Didn't they need experienced teachers, especially one who "for 13 months ... taught a colored school of some of Philadelphia's lowest classes and have considerable knowledge of their character"? As a precaution, Martha asked Johnson to send his response to a friend, not to her directly, lest the letter fall into her mother's disapproving hands.[4]

---

2 MS letter draft [to Oliver Johnson], Sept. 7, 1863.
3 MS letter draft [to Oliver Johnson], Sept. 7, 1863.
4 MS letter draft [to Oliver Johnson], Sept. 7, 1863.

In truth, Martha's experience teaching Black children did not reflect well on her, at least from the perspective of a historian. This was not unusual: even radical white abolitionists who, like Martha, believed in full racial equality held unconscious biases. In 1861, she took a position at the Bethany School in Philadelphia, replacing mid-term a teacher who had been unable to maintain discipline among her students. But Martha was a veteran; at twenty-two, she had already taught in several places. She knew what she was doing.

It wasn't an easy assignment, though. Outside, a group of white boys harassed Martha and her students. They threw open the windows and hurled in stones and sticks, screaming obscenities all the while. Other times, they threw rocks at the windows, breaking the glass. They rushed in the door and struck Martha when she tried to remove them, making her bleed. When these attacks happened, which they did more than once, she went to the police – authority figures who would have been eager to aid her, but not her students – for help.

I think here of the angry crowd member who threw acid on Melba Patillo as she tried to walk into Little Rock High School in 1957, of the white girls who dropped burning pieces of paper on her in the bathroom. Of Arkansas governor Orval Faubus, who used the state National Guard to block the Black students' entrance. Of the 1963 murder of civil rights workers James Chaney, Andrew Goodman, and Michael Schwerner at the hands of local law enforcement and other white supremacists. Of the Karens, the Derek Chauvins. White legal authority has rarely mitigated white vigilantism. More often it's been the same people. This was not Martha – far from it – but still: would her students have wanted her to call the police?

Inside, Martha prided herself on not showing her frustration, but she was stern, haranguing them to be good and

Crosshatch

instituting ever stricter rules. She also had a temper. She kept students after school, recording her frustrations in her diary as she sat across the room from them. She lectured them until they cried, for hours if need be. She tied their hands and feet together and secured them to the bench. On at least one occasion, she whipped them. Some, already fully grown teenagers, were too large to whip. They fought back, in what few ways they could. They sassed her; they insulted her; they hit or bit or threw objects at her after she punished them. In her diary, she revealed her true feelings about them.

They were ill-bred and neglected.

They were savages and brutes.

They were naughty.

They were mischievous.

They were impudent.

The students must have known that they frustrated her, that she could not conceive of their lives or understand why they behaved in the ways that they did. She tried to hide her pity when she visited their homes, but surely they must have seen that too, in downcast eyes or a ginger touch. It saddened Martha, a woman of modest means who was nonetheless accustomed to horses and help. She didn't remain at Bethany for the money, a meager $5 per week. She had offers to teach elsewhere for more, including one that her aunt Rachel Jackson had recommended her for. She did it despite her poor health and her family's objections. She did it because she felt called to.

In the end, she was sorry to leave. She thought she had done some good.

* * *

Like McKim and apparently Garrison, Johnson could not help Martha find a teaching position in the South. Francis

George Shaw, president of the National Freedman's Association, encouraged Martha to apply to his organization, though he warned her that they had received many applications from "competent and high-minded women" for only a handful of spots.[5] Perhaps this fierce competition for teaching positions explains why Martha did not receive an appointment until two years later.

Or maybe it was because she was alone. Philadelphia merchant Benjamin P. Hunt, vice president of the Pennsylvania Freedman's Relief Association, suggested as much. "Most of our teachers have some relation with them, as a superintendent or the like. There are no boarding houses, & so families have to be made up on some principle of relationship or previous acquaintance & arrangement to keep house."[6] Even Laura Towne, founder of the Penn School on St. Helena Island, had traveled with her friend Ellen Murray. There was no way, Martha learned, for a single woman to do it on her own.

As if that weren't part of the problem already. Martha needed a vocation in part because she was alone, but that aloneness proved an obstacle in securing a vocation.

In any event, in July 1865, James E. Rhoads shared the happy news that the Pennsylvania Freedmen's Relief Association had accepted her application. She would be heading as far south as the group could place her, which ended up being Rockville, Wadmalaw Island, near Charleston. It was entirely foreign to her family and friends. "I do not know where the island thee is on, is," wrote Anna. "How are the syllables divided? Wad – me – law? is it re or w[?] Is that right? I never heard of the island, and conclude it must be quite small."[7] After Wadmalaw she spent a year on Edisto Island and a year

---

5 Francis George Shaw to MS, [n.d.], in Oliver Johnson to MS, Sept. 11, 1863.

6 B[enjamin] P. Hunt to MS, Nov. 7, 1863.

7 Anna Webster to MS, Oct. 22, 1865.

Crosshatch

on St. Helena. In 1868, she began teaching at what became the Schofield School in Aiken, some twenty miles east of the Georgia border.

* * *

People always noticed the trees on Wadmalaw. In 1666, the eight Lord Proprietors of Carolina, then all of the land south of Virginia, sent Lieutenant Colonel Robert Sandford to explore the land that was suddenly, inexplicably, theirs. Sandford commented on the live oaks, the fields of maize cultivated by the Kiawah Indians of the Cusabo people, the level, sandy land descending to steep red banks. Historian Peter A. Coclanis compared the geography of the South Carolina low country to the scene of Percy Bysshe Shelley's "Ozymandias": "boundless and bare / The lone and level sands stretch far away."[8]

On June 23, 1666, Sandford formally claimed the land "by turfe and twigg" for "our Soveraine Lord Charles the Second King of England & c." Sandford likely stood in Rockville, the site of Martha's first posting in South Carolina, as he did so.[9]

Can you imagine, can you *even imagine*, everything else Sandford must have believed to think his actions made any sort of sense? The hubris, to begin with, the unquestioned assumption that the world belonged to him. Manspreading writ large, the entire globe claimed as easily as a subway seat, the rest of us smushed into the corner. Plantations came early

8 Peter A. Coclanis, *The Shadow of a Dream: Economic Life and Death in the South Carolina Low Country, 1670–1920* (New York: Oxford University Press, 1989), 13; Percy Bysshe Shelley, "Ozymandias," 1818 Poetry Foundation, https://www.poetryfoundation.org/poems/46565/ozymandias.
9 "Report by Robert Sandford Concerning His Voyage from Cape Fear to Port Royal, Jamaica from June 14 to July 12, 1666," Colonial and State Records of North Carolina, University of North Carolina, https://docsouth.unc.edu/csr/index.php/document/csr01-0047.

to this part of South Carolina. Between 1670, when the first English settlers arrived, and the end of the decade, as many emigrated from Barbados – wealthy planters and merchants and their enslaved and indentured work force – as from England. By the mid-eighteenth century, the South Carolina low country became a center of rice and indigo cultivation. The crops were labor-intensive, the still, humid air a perfect breeding ground for malaria and yellow fever. Even whites did not often see age twenty; demographic devastation was far worse among Africans and Native Americans. "I never thought I'd live past twenty / Where I come from some get half as many," sang another migrant from the West Indies to the North American mainland.

Old histories of Rockville pay a lot of attention to its twentieth-century yacht races, little to other kinds of races.

And/or racism.

On the eve of the American Revolution, the South Carolina low country numbered among the wealthiest areas in British North America. But the indigo market collapsed in the late eighteenth century, and South Carolina rice faced increasing competition from Georgia and abroad. Cotton took root only reluctantly in the area's soil. Wealthy inhabitants might not have noticed a decline in their quality of life at the time, but the area was primed for economic collapse even before the Civil War.

* * *

Rockville was in disarray when Martha arrived in October 1865, reminders of the recent war everywhere. "No one can imagine the desolation, the living evidences of Shermans Raid," she wrote of nearby Beaufort.[10] Rockville had been founded as a summer destination for wealthy slavers and their

10 MS letter fragment, first day eve 10th mo 15th 65 [Oct. 15, 1865].

Crosshatch

families fleeing the miasma of ill health further inland. Now, former slave cabins had been torn down for firewood. Formerly grand plantation houses lay decaying. Broken windows, discolored walls, overgrown lawns. Deer and wild horses ran wild. Martha felt no sympathy for the grand houses' former residents. She and her housemates had their pick of empty, abandoned houses. An especially cruel family of slavers haunted one of them, rumor held. Their land had once held stockades and other instruments of torture, buried as Union soldiers approached.

On long walks around her new home, Martha walked between fields where flames rose from the ground, devouring the tall grass and underbrush that had been allowed to grow, clearing the ground for something new.

It was several weeks before Martha began teaching. She, her fellow teacher Mary A. Sharp, Freedmen's Bureau agent H. A. Evans, and his half-brother Nathaniel B. Fisk, were tasked with aiding the 1,500 freed people who had followed Sherman. There was feeding and clothing the freed people, a daunting task. According to Cornelia Hancock, a fellow teacher who had sailed with Martha from New York, many of them only had one piece of clothing, a makeshift garment made from soldiers' tents.

There was setting up house. For a month and a half, Martha slept on a straw-filled mattress and a sawdust-filled pillow. A day with three meals was a rare triumph; one day Martha carried bread dough for half a mile to the nearest stove. When a boat bringing a month's worth of government supplies ran aground, Martha lived on crackers, and the freed people on dried acorns. But there was beauty there: the island was dotted with palm trees and orange groves, and from the house where Martha and the others lived, she could watch the sun set over the water. At night, she listened to the boatmen sing, their voices sweet.

Then, finally, there was teaching. She taught in another abandoned rebel house, spacious parlors now classrooms. Only one of her first group of students, which included twenty adults, could read or write. One woman brought her three-month-old baby. At school she found her students, sometimes seventy or more, many of the men former soldiers, "very attentive and I had no trouble, looked clean and neat, much better than I expected ... They seemed so eager to learn – it was a pleasure." This was good, because, Martha believed, it was their responsibility to "<u>prove</u> yourselves worthy of freedom." As a first step, she forbade them from using their former masters' names. She called her schoolhouse – every schoolhouse, until the one that bore her name was completed in 1870 – the Garrison School.[11]

"We have come to the wise conclusion, that we are exactly in the right place," Martha wrote home. The oaks, the moss, the warmth, the purpose made up for the dust, the desolation, the loneliness. Whether or not those at home believed her, she was quite happy.[12]

After a year on Wadmalaw, Martha moved to nearby Edisto Island, largely deserted save the ten thousand freed people who settled there after Sherman's march. Some had been forced to flee with their owners when the Union took Port Royal and returned with Sherman. Edisto "seemed like fairy land" to Mary Ames, a woman from Massachusetts who had taught there the year before, "everything so fresh and green – the air so soft ... the live-oaks in the background, with their hanging moss, had a very picturesque effect." A fine beach, by all accounts, though the river could be deadly. In May, the scent of wild grapes filled the air. Ivy ringed the house, clove trees flanked the door, and farther from the house were a Cape Jessamine and a white Crêpe Myrtle. Rattle-

11 MS diary, Oct. 24, 25, 1865, Apr. 22, 1866.
12 MS letter fragment, 10th mo 29th 65 [Oct. 29, 1865].

Crosshatch

snakes attacked plum trees, fig trees, hens. Ticks and fleas and mosquitoes attacked people. Smallpox ran rampant through the population of freed people. Missing windows, houses were "filled with sticks, plaster from the ceilings, and dirt of all kinds." The roof leaked when it rained. Formerly enslaved people, some back on their old plantations, used moss to wash dust from ceilings and dirt from floors for the newly arrived Northerners. Moss for mattresses, too, soaked in salt water for five days and then dried in the sun. In the local church, a half-mile away, a blown-out organ, empty window frames, doors hanging akimbo from hinges, pews in a state of wreckage. This was the first Freedmen's Bureau school on the island. "Hang Jeff Davis to a sour apple tree," students enjoyed singing in between their lessons. At the military camp three miles away, Black soldiers paraded for the newcomers in full dress.[13]

Conditions had improved by the time Martha arrived on Edisto Island in the fall of 1866, after a year of rebuilding. At the same time, however, President Johnson had pardoned almost all Confederates. Former plantation owners took back their homes, and formerly enslaved persons returned to their service.

Martha spent one more year on the Sea Islands. In 1867 she moved to St. Helena Island, where something like Reconstruction had been happening since 1862. Liberated after the Battle of Port Royal at the end of 1861, St. Helena and several other of the Sea Islands remained in Union hands throughout the Civil War. Union troops and dedicated abolitionist civilians arrived to feed, clothe, and educate the freed people in reading and writing, history and geography, basic science and math, and Northern free labor values.

Low and flat and gray, the coast of St. Helena reminded one observer of Tennyson's "Mariana":

13 Mary Ames, *From a New England Woman's Diary in Dixie in 1865* (Norwood, MA: The Plimpton Press, 1906), 6–7 (May 10, 1865), 10 (May 11, 1865).

About a stone-cast from the wall
A sluice with blacken'd waters slept,
And o'er it many, round and small,
The cluster'd marish-mosses crept.
Hard by a poplar shook alway,
All silver-green with gnarled bark:
For leagues no other tree did mark
The level waste, the rounding gray.[14]

The level waste, the rounding gray. Heathcliff on the moors, or Ozymandias.

***

The first teachers at the Penn School lived at Oaklands, a one-story structure bordered by a covered veranda, choked with weeds like the other abandoned houses. Oaklands had belonged to "Rebel physician" and notorious slaveowner Dr. Lewis Reeve Sams Jr. In 1860, Sams enslaved eighty individuals across his three plantations, with eight or nine families living at Oaklands. A woman named Celia told Charlotte Forten, who taught there in 1862–63, that "her master … was too mean to give his slaves clothes enough to protect them, and her feet and legs were so badly frozen that they required amputation." The Samses had left in a hurry after the Battle of Port Royal, decamping for Barnwell on the mainland and later Galveston, Texas. Medicine bottles, some of them still full of tinctures, lurked in one of Oakland's small, dark rooms.[15]

14 Alfred, Lord Tennyson, "Mariana," 1830, Poetry Foundation, https://www.poetryfoundation.org/poems/45365/mariana.
15 The National Archives in Washington DC; Washington DC, USA; Eighth Census of the United States 1860; Series Number: M653; Record Group: Records of the Bureau of the Census; Record Group Number: 29, accessed via Ancestry.com; Charlotte Forten, "Life on the Sea Islands, Part

Crosshatch

In a picture of the family taken in 1866, Sarah Fripp Sams, Lewis Reeve Sams's wife, holds an ambrotype of her son Joseph Edings Sams, who had died fighting for the Rebels the previous year at the age of sixteen. Another son, Dr. Calhoun Sams, survived the war as a surgeon under J. E. B. Stewart's command.

Did the Samses have any regrets?

The school itself was then located in a Baptist church, a brick building surrounded by oak trees, which were covered in a luxuriant gray moss so thick that it hung from the trees in webs some four or five feet long. Vines climbed the tree trunks and encircled the branches, crisscrossing the space between trees in a tangled green web. Part of the mile-long walk between Oaklands and the school went through the woods, the satisfying crunch of pine needles on the ground, the songs of mockingbirds above. The rest of the time the roads were sand, which grabbed and only reluctantly let go of one's feet. The school building had no chimney, and fires were impossible. Sometimes that first winter, the teachers held classes outside, where it was warmer.

Martha joined Laura Towne on St. Helena in 1867. Teachers on the island no longer faced the same privation Laura did five years ago, when a friend told her to "bring with me every thing that civilized life requires." Still, she warned Martha to be prepared: beyond a bed and a few other pieces

---

I," *The Atlantic*, May 1864, online at https://www.theatlantic.com/magazine/archive/1864/05/life-on-the-sea-islands/308758/. Charlotte Forten was a member of the prominent Forten-Purvis clan of Black abolitionists. In Philadelphia Charlotte moved in the same circles as the Schofields, and she and Martha must have known each other, even though Charlotte moved to Massachusetts in 1854, when Charlotte was sixteen or seventeen and Martha just fourteen or fifteen. By 1867–68, when Martha taught at the Penn School, Charlotte had left, returning north for health reasons. Charlotte later married Francis Grimké, son of Sarah and Angelina Grimké's slaveowning brother Henry and one of the women whom he enslaved.

of furniture, she would find little. School would be a similar story: few, if any, books would be immediately available for her students, who could number as many as one hundred. It would be just Martha and a chalkboard.[16]

Teaching on St. Helena, as elsewhere on the Sea Islands, was not easy.[17] There was no reason to think that teaching elsewhere would be easier. But malaria also ran rampant on the Sea Islands and elsewhere in South Carolina in the summer and fall of 1867, delaying the start of the school year and decimating the population of white Northern transplants, who lacked immunity. "Malaria everywhere," blared an advertisement in the *Charleston Daily News*, "a fatal element pervades the Universal Air this season."[18]

City boosters painted a rosier picture of public health in Charleston. Yellow fever outbreaks had emerged in other southern cities, but in the South Carolina capitol "we have enjoyed an unusual immunity from sickness, and the bills of mortality have been extremely light ... everyone looks forward confidently to a healthy season." When Martha passed through the city in late October, it had just emerged from a strict six-month quarantine. As far as officials were concerned, the future looked bright.

Regular citizens were less sanguine. "Since we left Washington," Martha wrote,

> the one subject of conversation with all classes has been the <u>sickness,</u> and <u>here</u> we hear of naught but the ravages of disease and the hasty work of death − . <u>Every white</u> person has been ill & many died with only two or three days illness ... so many in health a short time

16 Laura M. Towne to MS, Oct. 15, 1867.

17 Eliza Schofield to MS, Mar. 29, 1869.

18 "Malaria Everywhere," advertisement for Hostetter's Stomach Bitters, Charleston (SC) Daily News, Oct. 28, 1867.

Crosshatch

> before – . The cotton crop failed, the fever has stricken every household, & all are sad and despondent. We could not stay in Beaufort for the Hotel is filled with fever patients, even in Charleston faces looked white & deathly, moving about – .[19]

Martha felt an overwhelming sense of dread that day, as she approached her new teaching assignment, and within two weeks she fell ill: chills and fever, then coughing, congestion, and inflammation in her lungs. She began spitting blood. For two months – November 17, 1867, until January 16, 1868 – she could not write. For four weeks, she could not get out of bed, and even after that she had to be carried up and down the stairs. Laura stayed home from school to care for her, staying up into the night to read to Martha or bathe her head in cold water. When Lydia arrived at the end of December, Martha finally began to regain her strength. But she still spat blood every morning; she still could not sit for long periods without chest pain.

Martha never feared death, for her work was not done. Her students had lost so much time already, and some would soon have to return to the cotton fields. If I had been around to ask her, she would have said that her calling was more important than her life. But she also had no choice but to continue working, for she needed the money.

The illness (and heartbreak) of 1866–68, however, had worn Martha down. "This past two years has been too much for me," she wrote in her diary in April 1868, "My mind & heart have passed through such fiery ordeals, the frail tenement is shattered and broken – ." As soon as she left South Carolina for the summer, Martha began hinting to Laura that she might not return to St. Helena. The climate that Martha had hoped would benefit her health had attacked it

19 MS diary, Nov. 2, 1867.

instead. Perhaps Aiken, far from the coast, would be more salubrious. "The fine climate, the balmy air, the clearness of the atmosphere, its wonderful effects upon invalids afflicted not only with diseases of a pulmonary character, but those of an asthenic nature, … have attracted the attention of many individuals who have remained here for a longer or shorter period," wrote a city booster in 1870. New York newspaperman Thurlow Weed had seen "so many northern individuals improving in health and spirits that I cannot doubt that Aiken is as desirable a locality for pulmonary patients as can be found in Europe or America."[20] Walks to nearby Coker or Calico Springs or through the pine-scented woods could do wonders for weakened lungs. It was just what Martha needed.

Corn, wheat, oats, and fruits of all kinds grew easily in Aiken, animals flourished in the mild winters, and land was cheap. Labor, too. Clay deposits lent themselves to handcrafts that could rival those made in Europe. Far from the swampy, malarial lowlands that many Northerners pictured, Aiken was wooded and healthful, like the North but milder. It was safe, and clean, and orderly. One hundred and twenty miles west of Charleston, twenty miles northeast of Augusta, Georgia, Aiken lay on a watershed between streams that emptied into the Atlantic at Savannah and those that did so at Charleston.

It wasn't the South, not *really*, these writers implied, like my brother says about his home in Greensboro, North Carolina, not the lawless coil of bigotry and poverty that many Northerners, then and now, have imagined. It was not *Deliverance*, which I have not seen but nonetheless understand as shorthand for outsiders to make fun of the South. Northerners needn't fear for their safety in Aiken, as stereotypes held. "Strangers are *invited* and URGED to come and settle in their

---

20 MS diary, Apr. 29, 1868; *Aiken, South Carolina: A Description of the Climate, Soils, and the Nature of the Products in the Vicinity of Aiken, S.C. …* (New York: J. C. Derby, 1870), 1, 2.

Crosshatch

midst," boosters insisted. "In none of the other States of the Union – not excepting any – are the people better protected, or the laws more impartially enforced," proclaimed General John A. Wagener, South Carolina commissioner of immigration. Steamship fare from New York to Aiken via Charleston cost $22, no small sum, which indicated the sort of migrants town boosters hoped to attract. In addition to Northerners, Wagener appealed to immigrants from abroad, like the successful colony of transplants from his native Germany that he had established in Walhalla, South Carolina, in the 1850s. Never mind that South Carolina was only interested in Protestant immigrants from northern and western Europe. "We should have more people from Norway," its white inhabitants may have wished.[21]

* * *

Aiken County was not established until three years after Martha moved to the area, carved out of adjoining Barnwell, Edgefield, Lexington, and Orangeburg Counties, but the town of Aiken was named in 1835 for the first president of the South Carolina Railroad Company, which had recently connected the town to the eastern portion of the state. Aiken grew so quickly that the Bank of South Carolina established a branch there nearly immediately, the only brick building in the area. It was also the only building to survive a fire that ripped through Main Street in 1837, huffing and puffing its way through the dry pine edifices that surrounded the bank. A young man had started the fire, rumor held, in an attempt to smoke out a nest of yellow jackets threatening his litter of puppies. Fallout from President Andrew Jackson's Bank War soon ignited a financial panic, from which Aiken recovered only slowly. In 1868, when Martha arrived, the bank had

21 *Aiken, South Carolina*, 7, 8.

become a lawyer's office, surrounded by hotels, insurance agents, livery stables, bath houses, bakeries, drugstores, millineries, grocery and dry good stores, toy stores, liquor stores, hardware stores, and more. The town's thirteen hundred residents had many choices for where to spend their money. Effects of the recent war lingered, with dilapidated or abandoned buildings dotting the otherwise bustling landscape.

The region's longer history, too, lingered. At the turn of the eighteenth century, English skin and fur traders traversed the area, engaging in commerce with the Cherokee. By the 1750s, Aiken was part of Orangeburgh District, home to farmers of English and Scots-Irish origins, many of them former indentured servants. Fort Prince George, built near the Indian town of Keowee in 1753, became a symbol of English military might, intended to intimidate Native nations. Far away from the legal and judicial apparatus of Charleston, residents displeased with how officials handled Indian and other matters deemed themselves Regulators and enacted their own vigilante rule, taking on royal authorities in a battle that presaged the American Revolution; though South Carolina was a bastion of Loyalist sentiment, a large proportion of residents of Aiken and its vicinity served the Patriot cause. In addition to settlers from abroad, the area received migrants from the North, the Upper South, and nearby Georgia, the last group fleeing the colony's prohibition on spirits and slavery. Both were allowed in South Carolina. Around Aiken, cotton grew easily in the sandy soil, though Washington, traveling through the area in 1791, found it barren. Granite and millstone were abundant, with ripples of gold and copper.

Nineteenth-century local lore held, proudly, that Jefferson Davis was born near Aiken. He wasn't, but Confederate general James Longstreet was – a legacy that, like the war more generally, was of considerable significance to local whites when Martha moved to the area in 1868, in a season of radical

Crosshatch

social and political change. The Confederate cavalry under General Joseph Wheeler had met and matched Sherman in 1865, forcing him to abandon his plan to destroy the railroad, to retreat, and to find another route east. Aiken residents were just as determined to force Reconstruction to retreat. For over a century, class resentment toward elite outsiders, along with a belief that the government oppressed them to benefit others, grew among Martha's neighbors — resentment that they did not hesitate to express through violence.

CHAPTER NINE: WITNESS

In Aiken, late at night, Martha donned a bathrobe and lit a lamp to walk around the campus, always on the lookout for fires, dangers that arose naturally – and unnaturally. Once, she stopped a group of white men who had come to burn down the school. Another time, a group of local whites threatened to shoot her if she did not close the school.

Post–Civil War racial terrorism predated and extended beyond the Ku Klux Klan, which was founded in Tennessee in 1866 and first appeared in South Carolina in 1868, the same year that Martha moved to Aiken, but it became the most visible symbol of white resistance to Reconstruction. Donning white robes that evoked the specter of dead Confederate soldiers, at midnight its members, perhaps as many as a thousand in a very active county, marauded through southern towns with whips, knives, and shotguns. Whipping was the most common form of violence; gun violence the most deadly. Membership drew from all socioeconomic groups of White men, not just the poorer whites to whom racial violence has often been attributed. If anything, it skewed toward the elite.

As violence increased early in 1871, the federal government took action. The Enforcement Acts of 1870 and 1871 gave Congress the power to ban clandestine political organizations like the Klan. They also called for the formation of a committee to investigate Klan violence. In August, South Carolina governor Robert K. Scott offered a $200 reward for information leading to the arrest and conviction of any individual associated with the organization. In October, President Ulysses S. Grant declared nine South Carolina counties to be in a state of rebellion, then suspended the writ of habeas corpus in those areas. Federal marshals rounded up suspected Klan members en masse that fall, to be tried in federal court.

Martha saw a half dozen of them, all on trial for murder, brought to the federal courthouse in Columbia. Their own confessions made the friends who accompanied her, hearty men all, feel sick. Even the judge and district attorney needed to take breaks from listening to their testimony.

For all that the men on trial were willing to admit, some insisted on their innocence, claiming that they had never belonged to the organization or even that it did not exist, and fellow whites were often eager to believe them. According to John Witherspoon Ervin of South Carolina, "'The Ku-Klux Conspiracy' was one of the greatest frauds ever practised by a government upon a too credulous people." Many white Northerners, too, preferred to believe that the Klan was a figment of Black imagination than to acknowledge the systemic, totalizing reality of racial terrorism. John W. L. Tylee, a New York transplant to Charleston, South Carolina, insisted to a friend that "the Ku Klux Klan of which you lift a description from a Northern newspaper is altogether an imaginary organization." Tylee and others like him may well have genuinely believed this to be true. But it is also true that the Klan did not reflect well on the country, and so many simply chose not to believe that it existed.[1]

---

1 John Witherspoon Ervin quoted in Bradley David Proctor, "Whip, Pistol, and Hood: Ku Klux Klan Violence in the Carolinas during Reconstruction" (PhD diss., University of North Carolina at Chapel Hill, 2013),

Crosshatch

Martha had seen these horrors up close. While southern Blacks bore the vast, vast brunt of Klan terrorism, its members also targeted sympathetic whites, including those who taught Black children, and the institutions they founded, including schools. Martha knew that the organization existed and that its members were capable of the very worst. "If any one doubts the existence of such an organization," she wrote to her old Lyceum back in Darby, "let them come down here – and be willing to know the truth – ... The strong arm of the U.S. Law cannot give <u>more</u> than they deserve – ." No one knew the truth of these horrors better than the Black people targeted by the Klan. [2]

* * *

In September 1876, nineteen-year-old Molly Bush and her husband, Dave, were sharecroppers on land owned by George W. Bush (no known relation to the former president) in Ellenton, Aiken County. A little over a decade earlier, the Bushes had likely worked this same land as enslaved persons, and they may have been related to the white Bushes. At the very least, Dave and George had grown up together. Molly and Dave were newlyweds expecting their first child, and Dave had nearly completed his training to become a Baptist minister.[3]

On the first or second day of the month, George approached Molly and Dave in the field.

182–83; John W L. Tylee quoted in Proctor, 181.

2 Sarah to MS, Nov. 12, 1876; MS draft letter to Lyceum, Nov. 1871.

3 This account of the massacre itself relies primarily on Molly Bush to the Lawyers of Mr. George W. Bush, transcribed by MS, in MS, "Notes on Massacre," May 1877; MS to the editor, *Wilmington (DE) Daily Commercial*, Nov. 16, 1876; MS to the editor, *New-York Tribune*, Nov. 15, 1876; and MS, "Injustice in South Carolina," *The Woman's Journal*, June 23, 1877. See also An Occasional Correspondent, "The Southern Massacres," *New York Times*, May 25, 1877, which confuses some of the details of Hettie Kelsey and Mary Bush's testimonies.

Dave, he asked, *have you got a gun?*

No, Massa George, Dave responded, *I ain't got none.*

Then hurry and lay by your crop.

Bush, that is very strange, why did he ask, did you have a gun? Molly, puzzled, asked her husband after George had left.

I don't know — it is strange. The September sun continued to beat down as Dave and Molly resumed their work. Soon it would be time to harvest the corn.

Several days later, Dave approached George with a request: could he build a crib to store his corn in?

George assented, but with one condition: either to vote for the Democratic ticket or not to vote at all in the upcoming election.

Massa George, before I will do that, or stay home, I will suffer death. I am going to die a Republican man, exceptin' God comes and tells me not to vote Republican. The Republican Party was then the party of Lincoln, of emancipation, of expanded Black voting and citizenship rights.

Dave sensed danger but could not yet bring himself to believe what George was insinuating. *Massa George*, Dave asked then, *you wouldn't shoot me? We were boys and brought up together.* But the men's shared past meant nothing to George.

Dave, George menaced, *you are going to regret them very words you spoke. We aim to have this election, if we made for it, up to our saddle girths in blood.* Later, when George and ten other men were on trial for conspiracy, this was the phrase almost all witnesses for the prosecution recalled hearing: *up to their saddle girths in blood.* Hell-bent on bringing Reconstruction to an end, George and other like-minded white men did not care how many individuals — especially Black Republicans — they had to kill to ensure a Democratic victory.

I feel death, Dave told Molly, *I know they will kill me … Five months since we were married. I must pray God to make me willing to part with you. I am not afraid to die.*

George came looking for Dave the next morning.

Molly, where's Dave? he asked. Thirty armed men waited behind him.

Mass George, I don't know, he is off in the swamp. George pulled out his "dead list," which included the names of the men he and his posse planned to kill. Dave's name was on it. *When they came to my husband's name,* Molly told Martha later, *I was so hurted I can't remember the rest so well.*

After brandishing his list at Molly, George rode off without another word. He and his men returned in the evening, guns slung over their shoulders.

Molly, is you certain Dave ain't killed yet? George taunted.

No, sir, I know he ain't.

But he was. George had ordered it done, and he had seen with his own eyes Dave's body lying on the ground, riddled with bullets from his men's guns. Now, he offered to prove it to Molly, leading her past the cotton hatch and the white men guarding the body, to a spot near an old log and a persimmon tree.

When I went, she recalled the next spring, *I saw my dead husband shot under his ear, and it had taken out one of his eyeballs, and in his forehead, and on the head, his hands badly bruised, and his neck broken.*

In May 1877, the perpetrators of the Ellenton riot faced trial in Charleston. Despite receiving threats – including from George's wife – that she would be arrested or even killed, Molly appeared to testify against her husband's murderers.

I have given my testimony because it is right to give it she concluded. *They killed my husband, and if they kill me for telling the truth I am ready to die – , but if their deeds don't condemn them, I don't want them condemned – but I beg you to remember my murdered husband and my unborn child.*

Martha attended the trial in Charleston in May, hunched over her notebook, scribbling furiously as witness after witness confirmed and added to Molly's account. Martha had not witnessed the massacre, but at least two of her students had. They were picking cotton in the field with their father when a bullet whizzed by the two girls' heads. Their father had been targeted by white terrorist Red Shirts; he survived. In the months between the massacre and the trial, Martha had spoken with Molly and other survivors, and now she saw them take the stand. Martha was the only woman in the courtroom there specifically to bear witness to these women's losses, to the way they huddled together or fell to their knees, some with infants in their arms.

Hettie (or Hellen) Kelsey (or Kelsy or Kellsey), a twenty-four-year-old fellow sharecropper, actually heard her husband, Warren, murdered. The couple had been married for seven or eight years. Accompanied by Dave Bush and two other friends, the Kelseys had gone home for dinner after spending the day picking cotton. When a group of armed white men approached the house, the men ran toward the woods. Shortly thereafter, Hettie heard her husband begging for his life, even offering to change his vote. *I'se a good boy*, he promised. But the vigilantes shot anyway, killing Warren, Dave, and one other man. Hettie and Molly were too frightened to remove the bodies, which remained baking in the sun until the next day.

That same day, a posse galloped toward the home of Joanna Bailey, an elderly Black woman, and demanded that she produce her nephew. When she refused, two men jumped off their horses, sauntered into the house, and shot Bailey's nephew at close range. He died with his clothes on fire.

When the marauders came for Edward Bush, he stood on the porch with his wife, Mary, a child in her arms and two

Crosshatch

more alongside her. One refused to let go of him. *Don't kill my papa*, the child begged as the men dragged him off. Paralyzed with fear, Mary and the children may have seen Edward shot. She found his body a mile away.

* * *

The massacre in Ellenton supposedly began because two Black men, Peter Williams and Fred Pope, broke into the home of Lucy and Alonzo Harley, a white couple, and assaulted Lucy – a common trope used to "justify" violence against Black men. Despite Lucy's own insistence that they had the wrong man, a small group of neighbors shot Williams, who later died, and a larger posse of white men went after Pope. Allegedly, they found Black locals rising up in open rebellion. Over the next few days, white marauders killed one hundred Black residents. One was Simon Cooker, a Black Republican state senator, who was sitting at the train station when a group calling itself the Ellenton Rifles surrounded and executed him. In response to the murders, some seventy-five to eighty frightened Black men fled to the swamp, where they quickly found themselves surrounded by three hundred to four hundred heavily armed white men. Troops arrived to quell the bloodshed, not a second too soon.

In truth, the massacre was part of a coordinated campaign across the South to neutralize – either through intimidation or violence – Black Republicans ahead of the upcoming presidential (and, in South Carolina, gubernatorial) election.[4] The massacre in Ellenton came on the heels of similar unrest in nearby Hamburg, where white supremacist Red Shirts murdered six Black men.

---

4 Mark M. Smith, "'All Is Not Quiet in Our Hellish County': Facts, Fiction, Politics, and Race: The Ellenton Riot of 1876," *The South Carolina Historical Magazine* 95, no. 2 (1994): 142–55.

Former Confederate general Martin W. Gary had masterminded the plan of action. Democrats in every township must be prepared not only to control the official election apparatus but also to personally keep Black voters away from the polls by any means necessary. "Every Democrat," Gary argued, "must feel honor bound to control the vote of at least one negro, by intimidation, purchase, keeping him away or as each individual may determine, how he may best accomplish it." In a section of the plan that was omitted from the final written version but transmitted verbally, he even cautioned fellow Democrats to "never threaten a man individually if he deserves to be threatened, the necessities of the times require that he should die. A dead Radical is very harmless – a threatened Radical or one driven off by threats from the scene of his operations is often very troublesome, sometimes dangerous, always vindictive." Only elimination would do.[5]

Gary chaired the Democrats' nominating convention in nearby Edgefield that year. As one newspaper described the meeting, there "never assembled anywhere an equal number of more coldly furious men than composed this convention." Armed whites regularly interrupted Republican campaign appearances, sometimes in the hundreds. Pistols clicked to the ready if candidates so much as mentioned the recent massacres. In the end, Democrats regained control of the South after the election of 1876. In a number of South Carolina districts, white votes exceeded the number of residents who actually lived there. Amid violence, intimidation, and fraud, Reconstruction died.[6]

Strom Thurmond was born in this part of South Carolina. Lee Atwater, architect of late twentieth-century dog-whistle

5 Martin W. Gary, "Plan of the Campaign," 1876, in Francis Butler Simkins and Robert Hilliard Woody, *South Carolina during Reconstruction* (Chapel Hill, NC: The University of North Carolina Press, 1932), 566–67.

6 A. B. Williams, Columbia (SC) State, Aug. 15, 1926, quoted in Simkins and Woody, *South Carolina during Reconstruction*, 489.

racism, lived there from age five.[7]

Atwater was best-known for the so-called "Willie Horton" ad (1988), which drew on white fears of Black men as sexual threats to white women – the same myth that animated the murders of Peter Williams and Fred Pope, Emmett Till and the fictional Tom Robinson. "Tom was a dead man the minute Mayella Ewell opened her mouth and screamed," Scout learns in *To Kill a Mockingbird*. Seven years before the ad helped propel George H. W. Bush into the White House, in 1981, Atwater had famously explained the Republican Party's southern strategy:

> You start out in 1954 by saying, "N – r, n – r, n – r." By 1968 you can't say "n – r" – that hurts you, backfires. So you say stuff like, uh, forced busing, states' rights, and all that stuff, and you're getting so abstract. Now, you're talking about cutting taxes, and all these things you're talking about are totally economic things and a byproduct of them is, blacks get hurt worse than whites … "We want to cut this" is much more abstract than even the busing thing, uh, and a hell of a lot more abstract than "N – r, n – r."[8]

We were a part of white flight, I remember, that first level of abstracted racism.

In truth, of course, all of this started much earlier than

---

7 Strom Thurmond, senator from South Carolina from 1954 until his death in 2003, ran as the presidential candidate of the segregationist States' Rights Democratic (Dixiecrat) Party in 1948, while he was governor of his home state. A fierce opponent of integration, Thurmond also voted against the 1964 Civil Rights Act and 1965 Voting Rights Act. Republican political strategist Lee Atwater was George H. W. Bush's campaign manager in the latter's successful 1988 presidential bid.

8 Atwater quoted in Paul Waldman, "The GOP's Racial Dog Whistling and the Social Safety Net," *The American Prospect*, Mar. 14, 2014, https://prospect.org/power/gop-s-racial-dog-whistling-social-safety-net/.

1954 – much earlier, even, than 1876.

* * *

Of the 180 men initially held under bond for their role in the Ellenton massacre, twelve were charged, not with murder but with conspiracy. Eleven were tried, including George W. Bush. Astonishingly, the twelfth was excused because he was serving in the state legislature.

Judge Hugh Lennox Bond, who had presided over many of the Ku Klux Klan trials in 1871, oversaw the trial of the Ellenton rioters. In the earlier cases, Bond had promised to punish Klan members "even if it costs me my life." In his role as US District Attorney, Martha's friend William Stone, who later married her dear friend Mary, led the prosecution. Already in 1870, Stone had "seen enough of the South to sicken me with the crimes and brutalities committed on helpless negroes." During his tenure as Attorney General for South Carolina the previous November, Stone had spent two nights in jail rather than hand over election returns that he knew to be fraudulent. He was a good man and a good prosecutor. But the six white men on the jury refused to believe that Black witnesses were capable of telling the truth. The case ended in one acquittal, with the rest declared a mistrial.[9]

There is another term for this outcome: a hung jury. But it reminds me too much of Dave Bush's broken neck.

* * *

No single act provoked as much notoriety in Martha's life as

9 Hugh Lennox Bond quoted in Lou Falkner Williams, "The Great South Carolina Ku Klux Klan Trials, 1871–1872" (PhD diss., University of Florida, 1991), 108; William Stone quoted in Proctor, "Whip, Pistol, and Hood," 230.

Crosshatch

did her November 15, 1876, letter on the Ellenton massacre, which appeared in the *New-York Tribune*. In it, she laid bare the facts of the massacre, focusing on Molly Bush's story. Mail poured in, and newspaper reports were filed across the nation. Responses ran the gamut. Friends and strangers alike praised Martha's courage, even as they feared for her safety. "We all thank thee from the very fulness of our hearts, for thy courage and testimony, and pray that good Angels will preserve thee from violence and harm," wrote Rowland Johnson, a family friend from New Jersey. A New York City lawyer thanked Martha for the letter but warned, "<u>Be careful of yr. life</u>; do not be seen out at night." But perhaps these well-meaning men underestimated Martha. "I have felt anxious about thee," her friend Sarah wrote, "and yet have always quieted that feeling by remembering how brave thee was when the Ku Klux were around."[10]

At the other end of the spectrum, an anonymous piece of hate mail read,

> just Such Cattle as you, are the ones that keep up strife between [North] & South – Such lies as you wrote the "Tribune" 29th Nov is what is the matter – you knew every word was a lie when you wrote it – & thought you might get some notoriety by it. If you had lead a decent life at home, you might have remained there, instead of being forced to leave & come here to Vilify the southern whites – live with the whites & you will like them better.[11]

"Home" in this case meant the North, but it also resonated – as did "cattle" – with ideas about what women should and

---

10 Rowland Johnson to MS, Nov. 15, 1876; James B. Silkman to MS, Nov. 17, 1876; Sarah to MS, Nov. 12, 1876.
11 Anonymous hate mail to MS, Dec. 6, 1876.

shouldn't do.

Martha took such insults in stride. Her laughter rang out over a similar response: "The male who exhausted himself of words – certainly not ideas – can not harm my character – it is beyond his reach – ." How, she wondered, could this man possibly think he could scare her? One of her ancestors on the Jackson side had been burned at the stake in 1556 for his beliefs, "and in the 300 years since the blood has been true to its convictions of rights." Nearly four decades earlier, in 1520, family members on the Schofield side had been knighted in England for acts of courage. Martha had come naturally by her fortitude, and she would not be silenced by small men. "You are one of the kind that opposition to makes bolder," an admirer wrote accurately.[12]

* * *

Some of the most striking responses to the letter asked a question: was it true? Had Martha really written the words that appeared in the *Tribune*, and did the events they described actually take place? Could she write back right away to let the curious party know? Their Democratic friends did not believe the reports of violence that appeared in the newspapers, insisting that they were all Republican propaganda. How easy it was for some observers to dismiss facts they did not like, whether it came from a newspaper or a trial witness. Samuel Foster, an assistant district attorney in Rensselaer County, New York, wrote that "many of my democratic friends here at the North claim that all such letters are 'bogus' and were never actually written but gotten up for political effect, ... An answer from you will tend to convince some of the candid and deluded democratic doubters and result in some good to

12 MS draft letter to the editor, n.d. [Spring 1877]; John Mason Rice to MS, Dec. 12, 1876.

the cause of equal rights and eternal justice." From Iowa, W. A. Helsell wrote to ask "if the facts as set forth in that article are actually so? … Is it a fact that negros are thus treated in South Carolina?" An especially poignant response came from Ohioan Pinckney Lewis Bone. "I Write in order to get a few lines from your pen Signing the truth of this Letter So that I can convince Some of my friends that vote in favor of Such conduct at least who vote the Democrat tickit that Such Letters is not send North as a mear Lectionearing Scheem from some Abolishinest to get Republican votes," he wrote. Bone had enlisted in the Union army when he was seventeen, came through twenty-seven battles, and marched with Sherman, all of which he survived without a scratch. "I believed that God protected me because I Was engaged in a good course helping to free a poor Down trodden race from the lash of a people Worse than [illegible] but I see from the tone of your letter they are yet under the iron yoke of opresion."[13]

How could these facts be controversial? "Facts are facts no matter what may be written or said to the contrary," Martha observed. *Facts are facts. Facts are facts. Facts are facts.* To her, reporting on the massacre was a simple act of witnessing, as Quakers had always done. "I had often thought," she recalled, "perhaps I ought to write the truth." Perhaps it was her duty; after all, "there are many many conscientious persons seeking ~~the real truth~~, and desiring to know ~~what~~ the real truth."[14]

First she crossed out "the real truth." Then she stated it boldly.

---

13 Samuel Foster (assistant district attorney of Rensselaer County, NY) to MS, Nov. 18, 1876; W. A. Helsell (Iowa) to MS, Dec. 11, 1876; Pinkney Lewis Bone (Ohio) to MS, Nov. 26, 1876.

14 MS draft letter to the editor, 1877–78; MS to the editor, *Wilmington (DE) Daily Commercial*, Nov. 16, 1876.

Interlude: Not Even Past

The most striking feature of *I Am Not Your Negro*, Raoul Peck's take on James Baldwin's last, unfinished work, is Baldwin's brilliance. No other intellectual has articulated the interrelatedness of white Americans, Black Americans, and the concept of "America" itself quite the way he has. Nor, I think, has anyone diagnosed the sickness of white Americans with such stunning accuracy: we have become so disfigured, so monstrous, through centuries of inflicting brutality on others that the only way we can live with ourselves is through an utterly insane mass delusion of vacant, consumer culture–derived happiness.

The second most striking feature of the documentary is white monstrousness itself. It takes the form of white protestors in archival footage, shouting at and attacking children and teenagers attempting to desegregate schools or restaurants. The looks on their faces as they hold aloft Nazi flags and posters bearing racist symbols and slogans are so ugly, so menacing, so *knowing*, so *gleeful*, almost. This is the worst part of it, the part that makes me feel sick to my stomach: they knew what they were doing. They knew that they were depriving other people of their humanity, and they were *enjoying* it.

In Greensboro, my family and I went to the International Civil Rights Center & Museum, housed in the Woolworths where the 1960 student sit-in movement began. My brother and sister-in-law, who live in Greensboro, had been there before. They went the day after the 2016 election, because it was the only action they could think of to take that made any sense. People cried, they told me, tour guides and visitors alike. I am usually inured to the aura of historical documents and artifacts, but I was unprepared for the Klan robe, which stands alone behind glass, preceding a long, long hallway depicting more recent murders of Black men and women. I felt a sharp intake of breath, shivers, nausea. Disgust. Revulsion. This garment may have been worn when one human being murdered another. It was unlike anything I had seen before.

Those men covered their faces as they enacted their brutality: masks and hoods, signifiers overflowing with meaning. But their eyes, their eyes were enough, for that is where the monstrousness lives. Because what is monstrousness but the ability to look at another person and *not see another human being*? Cruelty lies elsewhere, as well: the jut of a jaw, a hand raised to slap or shoot a gun. But monstrousness: that is in the eyes.

I saw this look in recent years on the faces of the roving bands of sometimes armed white men patrolling city streets or protecting symbols of white supremacy. As I first drafted this chapter, in July 2020, angry white men tore down a statue of Frederick Douglass in Rochester, New York. When I was on social media, every year at this time all of my historian friends would post links to Douglass's famous speech "What, to the American Slave, Is Your 4th of July?"

Nearly simultaneously, a monstrous white man enabled by monstrous white men and women spoke in Tulsa, home to a century-old massacre of Black people and Black culture. At least two similar, albeit slow-motion, massacres were happening as he spoke. I cannot look at this man's face; I scroll past it when it shows up in news stories, which for years it always did, every news story, every day, everywhere. It is not because he is unlovely, though he is. It is because of the monstrousness. I can feel him looking at me, a woman, and refusing to see a human being. A white woman and thus a useful political pawn, perhaps, but not a human being.

In 2020, we could see their faces so clearly because they refused to wear masks, defying decency at every turn. They wanted us to see their defiance. They wanted us to know.

Did the roving bands of armed white men who tore through the South in 1876 have these same looks on their faces? I'm sure they did.

* * *

In the summer of 2020, the shots came so quickly that it seemed they had been fired by the same gun, which in a sense they had.

I had thought something was wrong with me – or, rather, that I was doing something wrong – by not watching the videos of police officers killing Black men and women. I thought I should do so to bear witness. This was especially true of Walter Wallace Jr.'s death on October 26, 2020, just blocks from my house in West Philadelphia. I should see his wife scream, his mother fall. Or was it the other way around? The media didn't report on the sequence consistently, and I couldn't watch it, so I don't know. But both women were there; both saw a man they loved murdered in cold blood. Dominique Wallace, Walter Jr.'s new wife, gave birth to their child just days later.

But Black voices caution against circulating and watching these videos, which bear so much similarity to snuff films, to the lynching photographs that sold for pennies as postcards.

"Black death has long been treated as a spectacle," Melanye Price points out. "White crowds saw lynchings as cause for celebration and would set up picnic lunches and take body parts with them as souvenirs. Their children would pose for pictures in front of swinging corpses, and those photos often became postcards." Why, these writers ask, is Black death not afforded the same privacy, the same sacredness, as White death – from COVID, from September 11, from mass shootings? "On Sept. 11, 2001, parents called into news stations around the country to ask them to stop re-airing footage of the planes crashing into the Twin Towers. News stations complied. Yet Black children got up and went to school this morning, and went to bed last night with video of a white police officer callously killing a Black man running on loop. What about *our* children? What about their sense of safety?" Brittney Cooper asks. Videos can change minds; videos can raise consciousness, some posit. But as Price, Cooper, and others note, anyone who doesn't yet believe in the reality of violence against Black people won't be convinced by one more video.[1]

It occurred to me that summer that the twin bodily ravages of 2020 – the slow, invisible deaths from COVID and the

---

1 Melanye Price, "Please Stop Showing the Video of George Floyd's Death," *New York Times*, June 3, 2020; Brittney Cooper, "Black Death Has Become a Cultural Spectacle: Why the Walter Scott Tragedy Won't Change White America's Mind," Salon, Apr. 9, 2015. See also Layla A. Jones, "How Viral Police Shooting Videos Can Mess with Your Mental Health," Oct. 28, 2020; Billy Penn; April Reign, "Why I Will Not Share the Video of Alton Sterling's Death," *Washington Post*, July 6, 2016; Sarah Sentilles, "The Viral Video of Ahmaud Arbery's Killing Shows Whose Deaths We Afford Privacy and Whose We Don't," Vox, May 11, 2020; Jamil Smith, "Videos of Police Killings are Numbing Us to the Spectacle of Black Death," The New Republic, Apr. 13, 2015; Allissa V. Richardson, "Why Cellphone Videos of Black People's Deaths Should Be Considered Sacred, Like Lynching Photographs," The Conversation, May 28, 2020; and Kia Gregory, "How Videos of Police Brutality Traumatize African Americans and Undermine the Search for Justice," The New Republic, Feb. 13, 2019.

sudden, public deaths from police brutality – were in many ways the same. Those of us frightened of riots or infection or both and with the privilege to do so could stay huddled in our homes like frightened cave dwellers, peeking our heads out to grab our overpriced, contactless delivery, safesafesafe and far away from the danger, while we let more vulnerable bodies risk exposure.

So much of it is about bodies. Protecting our own bodies. Determining which bodies deserve protection and which don't, which bodies pose threats and which don't. What other people's bodies can do to our own. The bodies figured as dangerous and scary are really the ones that are most vulnerable.

These were not two separate issues, not two crises that just so happened to crescendo at the same time. As Michele Norris pointed out in the *Washington Post*, "I can't breathe" applies in both cases.[2]

* * *

After June 2020, when the murder of George Floyd reignited the Black Lives Matter movement, Josh, my boyfriend, and I tried to be Good White People by consuming more Black culture. One night we watched *Just Mercy* (2019), which stars Michael B. Jordan as Bryan Stevenson, a young lawyer, and Jamie Foxx as Walter McMillian, the wrongfully accused death row inmate whom Stevenson defends. As a young child, Stevenson attended the segregated schools of southern Delaware, the region that those of us from the northern part of the state prefer to disavow, a microcosm of pretended northern innocence.

The film is competent but workmanlike, as the screenplay, based on Stevenson's own memoir, wanders frequently into

2 Michele L. Norris, "2020 Is Halfway Done. Let's Define What We've Just Survived," *Washington Post*, July 3, 2020.

procedural territory. But the performances elevate it above similar didactic fare; Jordan in particular lights up the screen (and may we all have the opportunity and the chutzpah to cast someone as beautiful as Michael B. Jordan as ourselves).

But the scene I want to talk about focuses on another character, Herbert Lee Richardson, a fellow death row inmate whose sentence Stevenson unsuccessfully tries to overturn. Richardson is a Vietnam veteran, and it is clear that he committed his crimes under the thrall of undiagnosed PTSD.

The film renders Richardson's execution in a series of dramatic but not graphic scenes: the long walk down the hallway, the fellow imprisoned men rattling their cell doors. I do not know what comes next, because I had to leave the room. Josh thought it was important that I stay and watch the whole horrific sequence, and I knew he was right, but I could not. I could not bear witness. I closed myself in the bathroom, and Josh told me when it was safe to come out. I returned to see Stevenson on screen, vomiting in the prison parking lot.

When Bill Clinton was running for president in 1992, he took time out from campaigning to preside over an execution, not to bear witness but to show how tough on crime he was. Ricky Ray Rector had committed the murders of which he was convicted, but he was also so mentally incapacitated that he asked to save the dessert from his last meal for later.

I am trying, as a white person, to learn how to write about race without falling into the easily available tropes: trauma porn, self-flagellation, a simplified morality tale of heroes and villains, triumphs and atrocities – in part because they're facile, in part because they can so easily be twisted to be about me, a white woman, about my unproductive white guilt, my ugly desire to prove that I am different from and better than.

Trauma porn is a tempting narrative, and certainly one that I admit I cannot entirely think my way out of. I do not want to reduce Black lives to suffering, but I do want to highlight the similarities between the Reconstruction and Jim Crow eras and today: the violence, the grief of those, especially women, left behind, the refusal of so many to believe in the reality of what was happening, mountains of evidence to the contrary. Can I do both? Does it matter? If evidence doesn't matter, as we know it doesn't to so many Americans, how do we change people's minds? How does change occur? The ugly side to this impulse is the desire to prove that I know how Black people have suffered.

Self-flagellation is equally tempting. White women are the worst, I could say (and surely have said) to anyone who will listen, all the while looking slyly out from under my eyelashes to see if my audience will tell me that I'm different.

Because, of course, if the history of race and racism is one of heroes and villains, I want to be one of the heroes.

For a short while after the 2016 election, we all (by which I mean Good White People) wore safety pins on our sweaters. The point was to show that we were safe people (by which I mean not Trump voters), like the rainbow stickers professors put on their office doors when I was in college — safe person, safe space.

As if we could control whether others saw us as safe, as if declaring that we were made it so.

Shortly after the election I got dinner with two friends from grad school, a married couple, one of whom was from outside Philadelphia, the other from outside Chicago. Their careers had taken them to Ames, Iowa, where their representative at the time was Steve King, self-described supporter of white nationalism and white supremacy. We talked about the safety pins then, agreeing that they were ridiculous even as we continued to wear them. *We're not like that*, the tiny accessories whispered, *We're Good White People*. How embarrassing now to think that our egos required this. I guess we all realized this, and the practice was abandoned as quickly as it emerged.

Is genuine, meaningful allyship possible? If so, what might it look like?

* * *

Poet Carolyn Forché has built her career around the concept of witnessing, stemming from her experiences in El Salvador immediately before that country's civil war. When she began writing about these experiences in the early 1980s, a segment of the poetry establishment balked: who was she to make poetry "political," to take it out of the realm of pure art and put it into the concrete, historical world? It was all right for women to write poetry, critics allowed, but their domain was the personal, the private, the subjective. Couldn't she go back to her earlier, lyrical mode of writing?

Another critique often lay just underneath this one: was what she said, were the atrocities she described, even *real*? In the late 1970s and early 1980s, few Americans knew about what was happening in El Salvador, and fewer knew of the US government's support for that country's oppressive regime, as an active misinformation campaign muzzled dissent.

What she said was true. She even published a poem that begins – and later a memoir titled – "What You Have Heard Is True." The poem describes the terrifying evening she spent at the palatial home of an unnamed colonel, which climaxes when he dumps a bag of human ears out in front of her. Back in the US, Forché found herself, as she noted in a recent interview, a Cassandra, speaking truth and yet not believed. She spent the next several years developing her concept of the poetry of witness, eventually editing two volumes illustrating these ideas.

All of the writers Forché included in these volumes had experienced atrocities. In her model, however, it is not the writer – or not *just* the writer – who witnesses. The reader, in recognizing a subjectivity other than their own, also does so. "In my sense of this term," she wrote in 2011, "it [witnessing] is a mode of reading rather than of writing, of readerly encounter with the literature of that-which-happened." Her ideas are indebted to many thinkers, perhaps especially Jewish philosopher Emmanuel Levinas, who spent most of World War II as a prisoner of the German army. "The witness witnesses to what is said by him (through him, or as him)," Levinas wrote in *Ethics and Infinity*, "For he has said 'Here I am!' before the other one; and from the fact that before the one other he recognizes the responsibility which is incumbent upon him, he finds himself having manifested what the face of the other one has meant for him." In other words, the response to "Here I am!" is "There you are!"[3]

So wrote Ariel Dorfman, who fled Chile after the coup by Augusto Pinochet in 1973, in his poem "Vocabulary," one of my favorites in Forché's first volume, *Against Forgetting*. "But how can I tell their story / if I was not there?" the narrator asks, "I was looking at them from another country / and I cannot tell their story." At first, it seems as if the narrator is trying to evade responsibility, but this is not the case. "Let me tell you something," the poem continues, "Even if I had been there / I could not have told their story." *Seeing* what happened — a more conventional understanding of witnessing — would not have been enough. Those who *experienced* events must describe them. "Let them speak for themselves," the poem concludes.[4]

---

3 Carolyn Forché, "Reading the Living Archives: The Witness of Literary Art," *Poetry magazine*, May 2011, https://www.poetryfoundation.org/poetrymagazine/articles/69680/reading-the-living-archives-the-witness-of-literary-art; Levinas quoted in ibid. This essay also appeared as the introduction to Forché's second edited volume, *Poetry of Witness*.
4 Ariel Dorfman, "Vocabulary," trans. Dorfman and Edith Grossman, in *Against Forgetting: Twentieth-Century Poetry of Witness*, ed. Carolyn Forché (New York: W. W. Norton & Company, 1993), 615–17.

When writer John Edgar Wideman finally, after wading through much bureaucratic tape, received the official file of the court martial and execution of Louis Till, Emmett Till's father, he found that he could not look at them, not really. "After an initial tingle of anticipation as I leafed through it, I couldn't bring myself to begin reading. Fear detoured me, fear and suspicion. Fear that too much is at stake. Or nothing at all. Suspicion of my motives. Fear of failure."[5]

I am further from the events I describe than Wideman was from his. Ever since I discovered Molly Bush's testimony in the archives, I have wondered about my use of it, the ethics involved. I knew it was the archival find of a lifetime: a Black woman voicing her own experiences in her own words, in a source that no other historian had used. But was it my right, as a white woman, to be the one to write about her? Did I do it for her, in pursuit of justice long denied? Or did I do it for me?

I have tried – like Forché, like Wideman, like Martha – to witness, to see in the uncrossable chasm of time and space and opportunity not an impediment to witnessing but its very nature. I wasn't there, and even if I had been, I couldn't tell Molly's story. Perhaps Martha knew this; perhaps this is why she did not editorialize Molly's testimony. *Let them speak for themselves.*

* * *

On January 6, 2021, as I neared completion of a draft of this book, I sat on the couch with the television on, work abandoned, jaw on the floor as day turned to night. "*Noch nie in mein Leben*" was all I could think to say, a favorite phrase of my grandmother's. Never in my life. Never in my life have I

---

5 John Edgar Wideman, *Writing to Save a Life: The Louis Till File* (New York: Scribner, 2016), 89.

seen such a thing. Never in my life did I *think* I would see such a thing. Inconceivable, incomprehensible. It's become a joke in my family because she usually used this phrase for things that happened *all the time* – never for the truly inconceivable, the truly incomprehensible. *Noch nie in mein Leben* have I seen ice skaters wear such skimpy costumes. *Noch nie in mein Leben* have I seen the Acme on City Line run out of Dannon coffee yogurt so quickly.

Not *noch nie in mein Leben* did I think I would be on a Red Cross train to Austria with two children under five, my husband a prisoner of war, bombs raining down on us.

Not *noch nie in mein Leben* did I think that, on Christmas day 1989 – the day of Nicolae Ceauçescu's execution – I would watch on television as a dictator was deposed in my country of birth, surrounded by my oh-so-American grandchildren greedily opening presents and stuffing their mouths with *Nusskuchen* and *Apfelkuchen*, not knowing.

I guess it was because these things really had happened.

I suppose it's my unshakeable irony, my inability to be sincere or show myself caring about anything, ever, that I appropriate this phrase now for something outside my ability to understand the world, something that lays bare the slow, inexorable tide by which a life becomes history.

* * *

Journalists didn't know how to talk about the people storming the Capitol: protestors, rioters, insurrectionists, terrorists, a mob. I still cannot wrap my mind around a titular head of state encouraging his followers to attack this same state. Political scientists have a term for this, apparently: an *autogolpe*, or self-coup, which happens, according to Wikipedia, when "a nation's leader, despite having come to power through legal means, dissolves or renders powerless the national legislature and unlawfully assumes extraordinary powers not granted under normal circumstances."[6] These events don't take place in flourishing democracies, but rather in places already drifting toward or in the throes of totalitarianism – the Marcos regime in the Philippines, for example.

Amid swastikas and smashed windows, nooses and guns, the image that stuck with me most from this day was not immediately violent: a white man walking through the building carrying a Confederate flag, passing between a portrait of abolitionist Charles Sumner and proslavery John Calhoun. These images are made for history books. I said this several times throughout the day: "these images will be in history books someday." The man looks like a normal dude, slightly red-faced, goateed, orange vest, baggy jeans. Your weird cousin, your boyfriend's stepbrother, the guy in front of you in line at a Wawa in *Mare of Easttown* territory. You avoid them at weddings and funerals and never see them otherwise, not that they want to talk to you anyway, uppity feminist killjoy in fancy-girl office clothes. This man, Kevin Seefried of Laurel, Delaware, eventually turned himself in to federal marshals in Wilmington. I've not been to Laurel, but Confederate flags do proliferate in that part of the state.

I said that this image wasn't violent, but of course violence inheres in the act of carrying this flag. Most of us know now, of course, that what we call the Confederate flag was never actually the national flag of the Confederate States of America – though certainly it flew over battles in which men killed to protect slavery – and that its widespread popularity dates only to the 1940s, when the Dixiecrats and other segregationists adopted it to protest the growing civil rights movement. It carries the Jim Crow era's violence in its fibers, too.

I can reckon with the flag as a symbol of hatred. I abhor

---

6 "Self-coup," Wikipedia, last modified Feb. 1, 2021, https://en.wikipedia.org/wiki/Self-coup.

Crosshatch

it, but it does not tax my cognitive abilities. What I will never understand is the flag's deployment as a symbol, supposedly, of patriotism. The men who first flew this flag were *literal traitors*. Those who carried it on January 6 *literally attacked* the United States. Yet somehow, they remain undaunted in their belief that they represent the real America, and that everyone else has betrayed its nature. Jefferson Davis argued the same thing. "If war should come," he promised in 1861, he was willing to "baptise in blood the principles for which our fathers bled in the Revolution."[7]

They are always so sure, these rampaging white men. In another time, Seefried may have threatened blood up to his saddle girth or screamed or thrown food at the young Black men and women walking into schools and restaurants. Look at their faces. Look at their anger. It just keeps happening.

* * *

I was too young and too white to pay attention to the Rodney King beating, the acquittal of the police officers who perpetrated it, and the unrest that erupted in Los Angeles afterwards. When I read Anna Deavere Smith's documentary play *Twilight: Los Angeles, 1992* in college, it seemed that the events her characters narrate had taken place long ago, though it had only been a decade, maybe less. Now I read about events that took place during Reconstruction, 150 years ago, and it seems as though they are happening now. Because they are. Before the beating happened, poet Claudia Rankine writes in *Citizen: An American Lyric*, "it had happened and happened."[8]

Rankine distinguishes between the *historical self* and the *self*

7 Jefferson Davis, "Speech in Montgomery, Alabama," Feb. 16, 1861, in *Jefferson Davis: The Essential Writing*, ed. William J. Cooper Jr. (New York: Random House, 2003), 197.
8 Claudia Rankine, *Citizen: An American Lyric* (Minneapolis, MN: Graywolf Press, 2014), 116.

self. In this model, one self comprises our individual, personal hopes, fears, and loves, while the other carries on its back the collective, accumulated weight of history, especially the history of race and racism.[9]

Actually — and I think she writes it this way intentionally — it is not Rankine but a friend who makes this distinction. Underpinning the entire book is the belief that the historical self and the self self are not different or separate. The past is "buried in you; it's turned your own flesh into its cupboard." *Or its archive*. The past is never past, etc. When *Citizen* first appeared, many readers assumed that the black hood on its cover alluded to the murder of Trayvon Martin, which had taken place just two years earlier. In truth, the artist of this 1993 work meant to invoke Rodney King.[10]

The illusion that the historical self and the self self are different is open only to some — namely, white people. Rankine notes elsewhere that white Americans are allowed to believe that they have no history, that they are born new and fresh and innocent. That's what *The Great Gatsby* — and so many Great American Novels — is about, isn't it? Escaping history, forging oneself anew? At the end of *Gatsby*, Nick ponders the "fresh green breast of the new world" that Dutch sailors saw in the island of Manhattan, "face to face for the last time in history with something commensurate to his capacity for wonder." Who is Gatsby but a man trying to make the force of his individual self stronger than the forces of history? But he can't, we can't. *So we beat on, boats against the current, borne back ceaselessly into the past.*[11]

White people certainly benefit from this historical amne-

---

9 Rankine, Citizen, 14.
10 Rankine, Citizen, 63, 72; see also Dan Chiasson, "Color Codes: A Poet Examines Race in America," The New Yorker, Oct. 27, 2014.
11 F. Scott Fitzgerald, *The Great Gatsby* (1925; repr., New York: Scribner, 1995), 189.

sia – no, it is not amnesia; it is willful self-deception – but we are the ones who walk through the world with compromised hearts, barely able to maintain our human form. "What the white writer might not realize," Rankine and Beth Loffreda write,

> is that she may well be an injured party – but the injury was dealt long before. The injury is her whiteness. By saying "injury" we do not mean to erase from view all the benefits and privileges that whiteness endows; we do not mean to invite an unwarranted sympathy. But we do think white people in America tend to suffer an anxiety (and many have written of this, James Baldwin most powerfully of all): they know they are white, but they must not know what they know. They know that they are white, but they cannot know that such a thing has social meaning; they know that they are white, but they must not know that their whiteness accrues power. They must not call it whiteness for to do so would be to acknowledge its forces. They must instead feel themselves to be individuals upon whom nothing has acted. That's the injury, that their whiteness has veiled from them their own power to wound, has cut down their sympathy to a smaller size, has persuaded them that their imagination is uninflected, uninfiltrated. It has made them unknowing. Which is one reason why white people take recourse to innocence ...[12]

It is the innocence which constitutes the crime. Baldwin, again.

Historians like to point out that the American dream is not upward mobility. It is self-creation. America, in this way,

---

12 Beth Loffreda and Claudia Rankine, "Introduction," in Rankine, Loffreda, and Cap Max King, eds., *The Racial Imaginary: Writers on Race in the Life of the Mind* (Albany, NY: Fence Books, 2015), 20.

is fundamentally ahistorical. Context, perhaps, is what Americans hate most. They hate thinking that anything but themselves determines who they are. I have never understood this.

Those most likely to appear in history books are also the most likely to argue that history has no hold on them. They insist that they are innocent of historical crimes; they reject even the existence of the historical self, let alone its constant presence. They will go to great lengths to protect this illusion of innocence.

Thus the 1776 Commission, a Trump-era educational initiative apparently intended to counter the silly idea that the history of American race relations does not reflect well on the nation. The commission's report, released on Martin Luther King Day in 2021, is a strange, paranoid document, which manages to discuss slavery almost entirely without reference to the experiences of actual enslaved persons, compares the early twentieth-century Progressive movement to Italian dictator Benito Mussolini, and ties itself in knots to connect the civil rights movement as it evolved in the second half of the 1960s to proslavery firebrand John C. Calhoun, all with a patina of Reagan-era faith-and-family discourse. I wish I could convey to you how *weird* this document is, how off the wall and sometimes laugh-out-loud bizarre is its strange obsession with identity politics, though that's not really the point. The point is that what the 1776 Commission and its advocates hate most is not Black people or women or LGBTQ persons, though they surely hate them, but rather the fact that we force them to see that we are all part of history, that we are not just individuals, that we do not simply create ourselves out of whole cloth, that our lives are shaped by forces outside of our control – including, yes, the groups with which we identify or to which we are assigned.

It's not so different from how I once thought of history: as something completely unrelated to myself and my experi-

Crosshatch

ences. It took me a long time to understand all of the other assumptions that informed this perception and made it possible.

The commission was dissolved by executive order early in the morning of January 21, 2021, the day Joe Biden became president.

* * *

Maybe it's all Hector St. Jean de Crèvecoeur's fault. "What then is the American, this new man?" the French American writer asked in 1782. He was, more than anything, *free*: free to cultivate the land, to reap the rewards of his labor, to live in egalitarian harmony with his fellow citizens. Free from the oppressive strictures, the bone-crushing poverty of European feudalism, along with its concomitant religious and cultural demands.[13]

Free to make himself.

Free from history.

Yet there's a reason some people called America "the best poor man's country." There's a reason I tear up at "The New Colossus" and Alexander Hamilton's dying words in the blockbuster musical from the optimistic Obama years: "America, you great unfinished symphony, you sent for me / You let me make a difference, a place where even orphan immigrants / Can leave their fingerprints." There's a reason I've dedicated my entire life to studying it. How absurd for anyone to think that reason is hatred.

* * *

Let's return to Cassandra.

---

13 Hector St. Jean de Crèvecoeur, *Letters from an American Farmer* (1782; repr., New York: E. P. Dutton & Co., Inc., 1957), 39.

Cassandra, princess of Troy, daughter of Priam and Hecuba, sister of Paris, can see the future. It is a gift from Apollo but a conditional one, given in exchange for her love. But she does not love him back, and so he curses her: she will keep her divine sight, but no one will believe her. Ever. Instead, they will think her mad.

Cassandra foresees the fall of Troy. She knows that the horse, supposedly a gift from the Greeks, is full of soldiers there to destroy the city. When no one heeds her warnings, she tries to take on the invading force herself.

When the destruction comes, she flees to the goddess Athena's temple and clings to a statue of the goddess for protection. Ajax, who leads a contingent of the invading forces, enters the temple, tears Cassandra away from the statue, and brutally rapes her, dragging her off among the spoils of war.

In her anger, Athena convinces Poseidon (in some versions Zeus) to stir up the sea so that it swallows up the Greek ships. Agamemnon, brother of Menelaus, brings Cassandra back to Mycenae to be his concubine and a handmaiden to his wife, Clytemnestra. He does not know that Clytemnestra is planning to kill him as revenge for his sacrifice of their daughter Iphigenia ten years earlier.

But Cassandra knows. In her "mad scene" in Aeschylus's *Agamemnon*, the scene every young actress wants to perform, she documents all of the bloodshed that has befallen Mycenae in the past, concluding by predicting two more deaths: Agamemnon's and her own. Clytemnestra is all too happy to fulfill the prophecy.

(Did Clytemnestra know of her own mother's rape by Zeus, I wonder? "The great swan, with its terrible looks, / Coming at me," wrote Sylvia Plath.)[1]

---

1 Sylvia Plath, *Three Women: A Poem for Three Voices*, 1962, online at https://utmedhumanities.wordpress.com/2014/10/13/three-women-a-poem-for-three-voices-sylvia-plath/.

I, too, wanted to play Cassandra. Actresses love mad scenes, the freedom they offer to express all of the anger and hurt we normally keep inside. But − and thank goodness − I am not a Cassandra: disbelieved, thought mad, raped, kidnapped, murdered. "They called me once, 'the prophetess of lies, / The wandering hag, the pest of every door,'" she confesses shortly before her death. In fact, the figure with whom I have always identified most in Greek mythology, despite or perhaps because of her close association with Zeus, with man-leaders like Odysseus, is Athena.[2]

Athena, goddess of knowledge but also war, literal embodiment of Zeus the father, trained from birth to value and defend his law and given so much of his power: could she use this power to defend the Cassandras of the world? Perhaps she is the one that those of us with power and privilege − people like Martha, like me − should try to reclaim. We're not Cassandras. We don't get the juicy roles, the dramatic monologues. Because we're lucky. But perhaps the witness of Athena can be bent to justice.

Let's stir up the seas to swallow Ajax whole.

---

2   Aeschylus, *Agamemnon*, online at https://gutenberg.net.au/ebooks07/0700021h.html#ai.

CHAPTER TEN: CITIZEN

In October 1854, some seven hundred suffragists gathered in Sansom Street Hall in Philadelphia for the Fifth National Woman's Rights Convention. The convention was an interracial, mixed-gender gathering deeply indebted to abolitionist networks; convention vice presidents included Lucretia Mott; Thomas Garrett, a famous white Underground Railroad conductor from Delaware; and Robert Purvis, a prominent member of Philadelphia's Black elite. A block and a half and seventy-eight years away, a group of white men voted to declare independence from Great Britain.

This irony was not lost on women's rights advocates. Convention president Ernestine L. Rose of New York claimed her rights "on the broad ground of human rights":

> By human rights we mean natural rights, and upon that ground we claim our rights, and upon that ground they have already been conceded by the Declaration of Independence, in that first great and immutable truth which is proclaimed in that instrument, "that all men are created equal," and that therefore all are entitled to "certain inalienable rights, among which are life, liberty, and the pursuit of happiness." Our claims are based upon that great and immutable truth, the rights

of all humanity. For is woman not included in that phrase, "all men are created free and equal"? Is she not included in that expression? Tell us, ye men of the nation, ay, ye wise law-makers of the nation, whether woman is not included in that Great Declaration of Independence? And if she is, what right has man to deprive her of her natural and inalienable rights? It is natural, it is inherent, it is inborn, it is a thing of which no one can justly deprive her. Upon that just and eternal basis do we found or claims for our rights; political, civil, legal, social, religious, and every other.[1]

Fifteen-year-old Martha and her mother were on hand for Rose's speech. "They went to the 'Woman's Rights Convension,'" Martha's fourteen-year-old sister Eliza recorded. A little over a week later, Susan B. Anthony came to the Schofields' home in Byberry for a sewing circle, and the next day eighteen-year-old Lydia went with Anthony and the Purvises to Newtown Friends Meeting, where Anthony spoke on women's rights. This family of women was perfectly positioned to participate in the nineteenth-century women's rights movement, in many ways an outgrowth of the abolitionist movement, and Martha became their most vocal advocate. When thirty years later Eliza too became a suffragist, Martha recognized that "the seed — of principles planted by a wise father and precious Mother" had borne fruit.[2]

Studying Quakers probably gives me a distorted view of how easy it was to be an abolitionist and feminist in nineteenth-century America. By 1861, Anna Dickinson, even younger than Martha and with a similar upbringing, was

1 Ernestine L. Rose quoted in "Proceedings of the Fifth National Woman's Rights Convention, Held at Philadelphia, 1854,"Women and Social Movements in the United States, 1600–2000, Oct. 18, 1854.
2 Eliza Schofield diary, Oct. 18, 27, 1854; MS to Eliza Schofield, Apr. 18, 1887.

a nationally known speaker. Martha heard her speak on "Woman and Her Position" in 1860, when Dickinson was just seventeen. "It was a grand sight to see one so youthful, one whose eyes shone from the brightness of the soul within, speaking so well and pleading so thrillingly for the cause of humanity," wrote the (apparently aged) then-twenty-one-year-old Martha.[3] But if feminism is still so controversial today, imagine how radical Martha and her family members – her whole community – had to have been.

* * *

Like most suffragists before 1865, Martha was an abolitionist first, and she prioritized this commitment. The subject of women's rights appears with more frequency in her writing starting in 1868 and 1869, at the same time that women were founding the nation's first national suffrage organizations. She was a founding member of the South Carolina branch of the American Woman Suffrage Association (AWSA), happy to have her name appear on the list of members and to pay the membership fee. "My whole sympathy is with the efforts to form a Womans Suffrage Association ... I am ready to have my name among the members. The 'entrance fee' will be paid just as willingly as the tax they demanded for my one acre of land, although it was a clear case of 'taxation without representation.'"[4] She refused to pay taxes otherwise. "I would gladly pay," she told state officials, "if they would let me vote." Her protest against taxes continued for decades. In 1895, fellow South Carolina suffragist Virginia D. Young praised her work to the National American Woman Suffrage Association. "Miss Martha Schofield, at Aiken, regularly enters her protest against paying taxes without repre-

---

3 MS to SB, Nov. 25, 1860.

4 MS letter draft to L. M. Rollin, Jan. 28, 1871.

sentation," Young noted. If only Martha knew about today's disenfranchisement schemes.[5]

Beyond the influence of her mother and her early exposure to Philadelphia's abolitionist-feminist milieu, Martha's time in South Carolina – especially her firsthand look at how men, particularly white men, preyed on, assaulted, and raped Black women – seems to have cemented her feminist politics. She took it upon herself to educate women on the dangers of the world. How men kept women out late at night and wore down their defenses. How women must be eternally vigilant. She worried over rumors about young women in her care, disciplining them if necessary. Just weeks after Martha arrived in South Carolina, she visited a young woman who was so sick that she was vomiting thick blood. Just fifteen, she had given birth to a child ten months earlier, tricked by a man who had promised to marry her. Martha feared for the young woman's death, and indeed she did not survive the night.[6]

As a social purity advocate decades later, Martha spoke frankly about sex, particularly the evil wrought by the long history of white men raping Black women. Under slavery, any children that resulted from these unions were legally enslaved themselves. Enslavers increased their profits either by stealing their own children's labor or selling them at market. "The market value of every coming child," Martha noted, "was calculated as a dairyman does his Jerseys." She never discussed sex in relation to her own life, except to insist on its absence, and she never spoke of it positively, excoriating white and Black men alike for not doing more to curb "ani-

---

5 MS letter draft to L. M. Rollin, Jan. 28, 1871; MS diary, May 23, 1868; Lydia Schofield to MS, Feb. 13, 1874; MS to Eliza Schofield, Apr. 18, 1887; Virginia D. Young, South Carolina state report, in *Proceedings of the Twenty-Seventh Annual Convention of the National American Woman Suffrage Association*, Held in Atlanta, Ga., January 31st to February 5th, 1895 (Washington, DC: The Association, 1895), 88.
6 MS diary, Oct. 27, 28, 1865.

malism." "How degraded men are," she often commented. As a result, in 1895 as fifty years earlier, "there are no young lives in America that have as much to contend with as the young *colored women*."[7]

* * *

Many white Southerners were perfectly content with this reality. Woman suffrage was a hard sell in the American South, where states' rights remained a cherished principle. Woman suffrage was a carpetbagger, imported from the North to destroy the southern way of life, the supposed superiority of which revolved around the elite white woman on her pedestal, of a piece with the indignities of Reconstruction and a threat to the project of Jim Crow. Southern chivalry, supposedly, would make it impossible for white men to prevent Black women from voting. "We are not afraid to maul a black man over the head if he dares to vote," confessed Mississippi senator John Sharp Williams, "but we can't treat women that way. No we'll allow no woman suffrage."[8]

As if chivalry had ever prevented white men from enacting violence against Black women.

Then too there was the fragility of Lost Cause manhood, tenuous in the face of defeat, requiring women's subordination to prop up bruised egos.

Sometimes I wonder how the Nineteenth Amendment was ever ratified. It seems impossible.

---

7 MS, "Slavery's Legacy of Impurity," in *The National Purity Congress, Its Papers, Addresses, portraits: An Illustrated Record of the Papers and Addresses of the First National Purity Congress, Held under the Auspices of the American Purity Alliance ...* Baltimore, October 14, 15 and 16, 1895, ed. Aaron M. Powell (New York: The American Purity Alliance, 1896), 175, 176; MS diary, May 9, 1868.
8 John Sharp Williams quoted in Marjorie Spruill Wheeler, *New Women of the New South: The Leaders of the Woman Suffrage Movement in the Southern States* (Oxford: Oxford University Press, 1993), 18.

Even Southerners who supported the extension of the franchise often did so as a way of maintaining white supremacy, with the votes of white women imagined as a counterweight to Black votes. Education or property requirements would ensure that only the right kind of women voted. No wonder the movement there gained momentum in the 1890s, amid the curtailment of Black rights, rather than the 1850s, as it had in the North. On the cover of its inaugural issue in October 1914, the *New Southern Citizen*, a publication of the Southern States Woman's Suffrage Conference, included a map of the United States that depicted states where women were enfranchised in white and states in which they were not in black. "Make the Southern States White," the caption reads.[9]

To be fair, many northern suffragists were perfectly willing to go along with this rationale, which was first proposed by former abolitionist Henry Blackwell, of all people. National suffrage organizations promoted the idea vigorously. Still others simply demanded gratitude from the formerly enslaved for what white women had supposedly done for them. White suffragists were fond of arguing that their work was "not for ourselves alone," a phrase that has since become the title of several books and a documentary. Often, though, they really were in it for themselves and their own advancement alone, as white feminists frequently still are.

Anyway, most southern whites preferred a direct approach to disenfranchisement; easier to "get out the shotguns and stand by the polls" than "use fair and lovely womanhood" as a bulwark, as one South Carolina politician put it.[10]

They were doing it for women, after all, for "the White Goddess of Democracy – the White Womanhood of the State,"

---

9 "Votes for Women a Success: The Map Proves It," *New Southern Citizen*, Oct. 1914.
10 Quoted in Wheeler, *New Women of the New South*, 18.

according to Charles Brantley Aycock of North Carolina.[11]

South Carolina finally ratified the Nineteenth Amendment in 1969. Mississippi was last, in 1984.

* * *

The first woman suffrage organization in South Carolina was founded in 1870, its membership consisting of white women from the North and African Americans like the Rollin sisters, the driving force behind the South Carolina AWSA. Martha was close with three of them: Charlotte (Lottie), Katherine (Katie), and Frances. All three had experience teaching in schools for freed people. Martha may have known Frances Rollin as early as 1859, when Frances convinced her father to let her attend school in Philadelphia. Out of their home in Charleston, a "commodious, well-appointed house located in a fashionable residential section near the state capitol building" with "double parlors, exquisite furnishings, tasteful paintings, plush carpets, and extensive library," the sisters ran a salon for the movers and shakers in South Carolina Republican politics. In 1867, Frances successfully sued a steamboat captain for refusing her first-class passage, in violation of military orders. Beautiful, witty, and fiercely knowledgeable, the sisters often won over even their political opponents. As a reporter in the anti-Reconstruction New York *Sun* noted, "their manners were refined, their conversation unusually clever and their surroundings marked them as ladies of keen taste and rare discernment. But for their color they might move in the highest circles of Washington and New York Society."[12]

Charlotte first called for women's voting rights in front of

---

11 Charles Brantley Aycock quoted in Wheeler, *New Women of the New South*, 18.

12 New York Sun, Mar. 29, 1871.

the state house of representatives in 1869. Women should be allowed to vote, she argued the next year, "not as a favor, not as a privilege, but as a right based on the grounds that we are human beings and as such entitled to all human rights." They organized a women's rights convention in Columbia in 1870, with Lottie as chair, Katie as secretary, and Governor Robert K. Scott, the anti-Klan crusader, in an honorary role as president. Scott's wife, according to Martha a "whole-souled woman," also joined the sisters' campaign for women's voting rights.[13]

In 1872, the Rollin sisters and their male allies called for the state constitution to be amended to include woman suffrage – a debate so explosive that it caused a fist fight among politicians. The measure failed, and over the next few years, the last of Reconstruction, the changing political climate made further activism untenable. At least three of the five Rollin sisters eventually moved farther north, to Brooklyn and Washington, DC.[14]

* * *

In 1878, at Susan B. Anthony's request, Martha attended a meeting of the National Woman Suffrage Association (NWSA) in Rochester, New York, for the thirtieth anniversary of the Seneca Falls convention, in a Unitarian church decorated to make the Flower City proud. "What a pleasure it would afford us, to see & hear one who has stood at the front of the army of freedom and equality at the south all these years," Anthony wrote to Martha. Southern women were

13 "Gossip from the Capital," Charleston (SC) Daily News, Nov. 12, 1872; Charlotte and Frances Ann Rollin quoted in William Gatewood Jr., "'The Remarkable Misses Rollin': Black Women in Reconstruction South Carolina," The South Carolina Historical Magazine 92, no. 3 (1991): 181.
14 Charlotte Rollin quoted in "Woman Suffrage Movement," Woman's Journal, Feb. 25, 1871.

Crosshatch

underrepresented in the movement, as the famous suffragist made clear. "Our great need is acquaintance with southern women" who supported the cause. It could be "so very lonely in suffrage work in South Carolina," Virginia D. Young wrote years later. As one of this group's few representatives and the only delegate from South Carolina, Martha became something of a celebrity. [15]

It was the last convention that Lucretia Mott attended, against her family's wishes. Halfway through her speech, her nephew begged her to stop. She descended from the stage, still speaking, shaking hands with members of the standing audience. "Good-by, dear Lucretia!" Frederick Douglass called after her. William Lloyd Garrison died shortly after writing a congratulatory letter to the conveners at the end of June. In another decade, Elizabeth Cady Stanton speculated in her opening address, all of the members of this generation of activists might be gone. Martha did not know life without many of them.[16]

It was a strange convention in certain ways. Stanton, a former abolitionist, quoted Jefferson Davis to argue that "a Caesar could not subject a people fit to be free, nor could a Brutus save them if they were fit for subjugation."[17] Or perhaps not so strange, coming after Reconstruction's end, and from a woman whose anger at being excluded from the Fifteenth Amendment made it impossible for her to support expanded Black rights.

---

15 Susan B. Anthony to MS, June 20, 1878; Virginia D. Young, "Woman Suffrage in South Carolina," *Woman's Journal*, Mar. 12, 1892.

16 National Woman Suffrage Association, thirtieth anniversary meeting report, in *History of Woman Suffrage*, vol. 3: *1876–1885*, ed. Elizabeth Cady Stanton, Susan B. Anthony, and Matilda Joslyn Gage (Rochester, NY: Charles Mann, 1887), 125.

17 National Woman Suffrage Association, thirtieth anniversary meeting report, 118.

**

By the 1890s, another constituency had joined the suffrage fold: native-born white women, many of them drawn from the ranks of temperance. They were often quick to insist on their loyalty to the state. In a speech before the state Woman's Christian Temperance Union, activist Virginia D. Young noted that "I am a South Carolinian, and have spent nearly my whole life within a hundred miles of Columbia. I was reared with the same ideas you have. My ancestors came to South Carolina from France, and have always lived here, yet I have believed in woman suffrage since I first examined the question, before I ever saw the North, or knew its people."[18] Along with Adelaide Viola Neblett, Young organized a small women's rights conference in Greenville, South Carolina, in 1890. In 1892, Young became state vice president of NAWSA and president of the South Carolina Equal Rights Association (SCERA), which advocated suffrage only for women who met an educational requirement. SCERA drew its original sixty members from nineteen towns, including Aiken, though there's no evidence that Martha participated. In 1893, as the South Carolina legislature debated woman suffrage for the first time, suffragists covered the desk of Robert R. Hemphill, the bill's sponsor, with flowers. Two hundred women filled the gallery. The measure was defeated, 21 to 14. Young was not afraid to use the argument that educated, property-owning white women's votes would overwhelm Black votes in the state, including during the 1895 state constitutional convention and in front of the Woman Suffrage Committee of the US Senate the following year. This, she believed, was the strategy for success. It was a "slow, up-stream propelling of the woman's equality boat in my state," she commented that same year, but "we are coming up like a thicket of pines, very small in our

18 Young, "Woman Suffrage in South Carolina."

Crosshatch

beginnings, but intending to be giants afterwhile."[19]

* * *

In February 1895, Martha hosted Anthony on her very first visit to South Carolina. The famous suffragist stayed in the parlor bedroom decorated with a new rug Martha had purchased in Philadelphia. It was cold and snowy during Anthony's visit, and Martha set up a coal fire for her friend, supplemented by some fat logs to keep the room warm. With little time to plan, Martha organized a meeting. It stormed the day Anthony was to speak, yet despite the weather and the short notice, the room was fuller than Martha had ever before seen it. Both the women and men in attendance sat in rapt attention as Anthony revealed the machinations of political parties, both of which excluded the very people doing the most to improve humanity – women. Anthony's speech was so well-received that the NWSA sent two organizers to the state ahead of its planned late summer constitutional convention. Martha and Anthony did not keep in regular touch, but four years later Anthony remembered her visit to South Carolina with pleasure.[20]

Sadly, but not surprisingly, the convention did not enact woman suffrage. Only 26 of 147 delegates voted in favor of the measure, which included property and educational qualifications. Indeed, the convention restricted rather than expanded voting rights, formalizing the Jim Crow disenfranchisement scheme that would reign for the next seventy years. Martha did not live to see either of her home states, Pennsylvania or South Carolina, grant women the right to vote, and in her will, she set aside money for the school library to

---

19 Young, South Carolina state report, 86.
20 MS to sister(s), ca. Feb. 15, 1895; MS note, n.d. [Mar. 1906]; Susan B. Anthony to MS, Dec. 19, 1898.

acquire publications supporting suffrage and equal rights for women. By the time the Nineteenth Amendment was ratified in 1920, southern segregationists did not need white women's votes to cancel out Black men's: poll taxes, literacy tests, and rampant voter intimidation had taken care of that.

* * *

This narrative of Martha's suffrage activism makes her feminism seem narrow, cut off from the rest of her life and with a disproportionate focus on formal political rights. Martha, I think, would have preferred it this way, for reasons that will become clear.

Decades earlier, in November 1872, Lottie and Katie Rollin hosted a meeting of the South Carolina Woman Suffrage Association at their home in Charleston with Governor Scott presiding. The assembly unanimously selected Martha as a delegate to the organization's national convention in St. Louis. Scott and Katie Rollin wrote her that same day to give her the news, but Martha demurred the honor. "While acknowledging the compliment of being chosen a delegate to the Womans Rights Convention at St. Louis," she wrote formally, "I regret that pressure of duties and combination of circumstances, will prevent my attending."[21]

She was busy. But I can't help but think that her decision not to go to St. Louis reflected something other than duty, something other than politics. I can't help but think it had something to do with who was there.

For Scott, you see, had broken her heart. Her personal and political lives were intertwined, much as she may have protested.

---

21 R. K. Scott and Katie E. Rollin to MS, Nov. 11, 1872; MS draft letter [to R. K. Scott and Katie E. Rollin], n.d. [1872].

CHAPTER ELEVEN: THE GENERAL

In the years that she grew more involved in politics, Martha came to terms with the fact that her personal life had not turned out as she had hoped. Her life in the North had included two great loves – John and Sadie – both of whom married other friends. In South Carolina, another possibility presented itself: General Robert K. Scott, the state's Reconstruction governor. Born in Armstrong County, Pennsylvania, in 1826, Robert Kingston Scott was thirteen years Martha's senior. He studied medicine before joining the army at the beginning of the Mexican-American War, in 1846. He eventually settled in Napoleon, Ohio, where in 1854 he married Rebecca J. Lowry. He and Rebecca had a son, Robert K. (Arkie) Scott Jr., in October 1865, and a daughter who died in childhood. Until the Civil War broke out, he ran a successful medical practice, alongside which he ventured into business.

During the Civil War, he rose to the rank of major-general. He saw action at Vicksburg and with General William T. Sherman in Atlanta and the Carolinas. One battle saw him enter with six hundred men and emerge with only 186, the rest dead or wounded. Briefly held prisoner by the Confederate army, he escaped with a lung injury and a lifelong cough. By the time Martha met the general in early 1866, he was traveling through South Carolina as assistant commissioner of the Freedmen's Bureau. He then served as that state's Reconstruction governor for two terms, from 1868 until 1872.

He seems an odd choice for Martha to have fallen in love with: a husband and father, a pugilist with a reputation for brutality and a politician with a propensity for scandal. According to an unsympathetic Jim Crow–era history, "he was notoriously weak and pliant and was incapable of withstanding the cool and deliberate strategy of his associates. He was 'subject alike to alcoholic and female allurements,' and on one occasion the scheming state officials gave a star of the burlesque stage a percentage commission to induce the drunken governor to sign an issue of bonds." As governor, he cracked down on the Ku Klux Klan, which once had threatened to "insure him a free ticket to Hell Station on the Devil's R. R.," and he worked to rebuild state infrastructure. But accusations of financial irregularity also plagued his tenure. His opponents attempted impeachment and once formally charged him with breach of trust and conspiracy, though these charges were eventually dropped. Later, back in Ohio, he was tried and acquitted of murder in the death of his son's friend Warren G. Drury.[1]

An odd choice indeed.

Looking at his photograph now, I see that he was vaguely handsome in that nineteenth-century way of vacant eyes and the facial hair of a Brooklyn hipster circa 2009. His hair is curly, and he's wearing his army uniform. The photograph does not show that he was an imposing 6'2".

"It was love at first sight with him," Martha confessed to her niece Polly decades later, "and I felt – that <u>first</u> day – a part – of me go out – that – never came back."[2]

I wish I could stop him from breaking her heart. *You're*

---

1 "The Impeachment Movement," *Charleston Daily News*, Dec. 20, 1871; "Death of Ex-Gov. Scott," *Baltimore Sun*, Aug. 14, 1900.

2 MS to Polly, Jan. 19, 1913.

Fig. 8: Mathew B. Brady, "Gen. R. K.[?] Scott, U.S.A.," ca. 1855–65, Brady-Handy photograph collection, Prints and Photographs Collection, Library of Congress, https://www.loc.gov/pictures/item/2017895996/.

too good for him, I would tell her. It's true. Both John and Sadie would have been better matches. John was more like a modern man, interested in poetry and music, someone you could go to brunch and the farmers' market with, someone with strong opinions about Bernie Sanders. Sadie, sweet and cheerful, was not Martha's intellectual equal, but she lit up the lives of those who knew her. Martha herself was unconventional. Wouldn't she have preferred an unconventional love? But perhaps she was breaking so many rules herself that she could not imagine being in a relationship with someone who was also doing so. It can be easier to change one's politics than to change one's life.

* * *

Martha's relationship with the general was professional at first. In February of 1866, the former Confederate whose house Martha and her compatriots were using for a school wanted to reclaim it, and under Andrew Johnson's forgiving Reconstruction regime, nothing prevented him from doing so. In his role as assistant commissioner of the Freedman's Bureau, Scott offered to find them a new house to use.

Quickly their connection blossomed into friendship, though I don't know how or when. Martha tore out the page of her diary immediately preceding her first mention of the general, which is impersonal. She did so again in April, and again, just a section this time, neatly excised, later that month.

I wonder when she removed these sections. Immediately after their relationship's ambiguous end, when, it seems, she burned many of their letters? Or decades later, as an old woman, hands shaking?

I'm glad I first read her diaries in physical form, where I noticed the alterations immediately. They're not nearly as visible in digital form. This is too bad, because absence provides

Crosshatch

a clue. *2 years ago in a little room – kid glove – ...* wrote Martha on April 8, 1868. Her diary entry for the same date two years ago is cut out. Perhaps this was the day that the general spent two days and one night traveling to visit her on Wadmalaw, spending $250 on a steamer to make it to the island. They sat chastely on an old sofa, quiet declarations of love filling the once-grand parlor.

Why did you love me so soon after we met? she asked him.

You gave me higher ideals of woman and more faith in God, he replied. *Be a brave restful girl for my sake and take all your duties slowly and do not worry about anything. I am loving you enough for you to live on without using a bit of your strength. Just draw on me for supplies of love comfort sympathy and repose. I love you.* He sounds not unlike the heroes of the romance novels I devoured as a teenager, which in turn were not unlike the ideals Martha internalized from the culture of her time. This is the promise of heteropatriarchal romance – the exchange of autonomy for protection. It rarely works out this way.

"He did not – even touch me," Martha recalled decades later, "and yet – I knew part of me had gone to him forever." She remembered this visit, and thought about him every day, for the rest of her life. Forty-seven years later, in 1913, she still maintained that "no daylight – has gone into darkness and returned – again that I have not thought – of him as present – with me ... You that are mated in this world know little of the – hidden chambers in womens hearts."

Once he seemed to feel the same. "God made your soul for mine and my soul for yours and we will be one through all eternity," he told her. The next few months were lovely and gay, full of shared outings and deepening feelings. In May the general took Martha and her friends to see Fort Sumter, where the first shots of the Civil War were fired. How kind of him to take them to a place so laden with solemnity, Martha thought. It was just the sort of outing she would have chosen for herself. At the end of June, shortly before she returned North for the summer, he gave her a parting gift of perfume and a traveling trunk.[3]

June in South Carolina meant heat, and it meant humidity, and it meant mosquitoes. Scott stayed at the house that night, and he and the house's residents had to contend with the pests. Martha and the three other women tried to sleep on the floor, eventually resorting to setting old magazines on fire in an attempt to smoke the mosquitoes out. The men, including Scott, stayed on the veranda, where he wrapped his head in a mosquito net. Everything was lively, and laughter abounded. It may have been the closest Martha ever slept to a man to whom she wasn't related, separated only by the front door. Did she think about him as she lay there, swatting at mosquitoes?

The next morning, Martha and the general walked to the wharf, where they waited for the ship that would take them off the island and talked.

I think I will miss you very much, he told her. She believed him but thought his feelings circumstantial. He was alone in South Carolina, without friends and family and laden with responsibility. But "coming to our Island Home, he found a free, open candid child, for he <u>has</u> certainly found my child-nature, & all my talk with him is unstudied, and natural – . Just right out of my heart, and without much thinking – ." She was twenty-seven, not so very young but still naïve, and she felt safe in this role. "I have always felt a sense of <u>protection</u>, with him," she admitted, a rest from the doubts that mostly throng around me, when meeting those here."[4]

Two days later, back on the South Carolina mainland, the general took her in a carriage to Magnolia Cemetery. They walked alone to a secluded bank by the water and looked

3 MS to Polly, Jan. 19, 1913; MS diary, May 9, 12, 13–22, June 24, 1866.
4 MS diary, June 25, 1866.

Crosshatch

toward Charleston in the distance. Hidden from view under a moss-covered oak tree, they expressed their feelings.

I know you better than you know yourself, he told her.

I see straight through you to your very nature, she replied. Such candor was the basis of their friendship. Friendship: this is how she always described it at the time, at least in the sections of her diary that she did not cut out. If she acknowledged more, perhaps it was on June 25, or 26, or 27–29, or 30.

Or July 6 or 7.

Or July 8. Four days earlier Martha had reunited with Sadie in Chappaqua, where they had vacationed seven years earlier. On the morning of the eighth, she woke at four-thiry, sitting by an open window to watch the sun rise. She began a letter to Scott, letting the words and emotions flow with "a childs trusting faith."

Martha never mentioned Scott by name in this entry, identifying her interlocutor only as "my friend." Or she did, but it's buried in the brackets and ellipses that punctuate my transcription of the day's diary entry.

> *I be*gan my letter to [cut out] …
>
> The quiet peacefulness of so early a sabbath filled my mind [cut out] …
>
> This is the *anniversary of my friends birth-day* [cut out] …

It's more than enough for the historian-detective. July 8, 1866, was Scott's fortieth birthday.

* * *

Martha's relationship with Scott continued to grow when she returned to South Carolina in the fall of 1866. She wrote to her sisters to tell them how happy she was to be reunited with him, her one true friend in the South. "Thee cannot tell my dear Mart," her sister Lydia wrote, "what a satisfaction it was to learn thee had found thy friend <u>General</u> <u>Scott</u> it must have been so pleasant to feel thee had <u>one</u> friend in that far off land and doubtless it removed or lessened the feeling of loneliness or homesickness." How lucky he was, too:

> Did any gentleman ever know my noble sister intimately without being benefitted, the influence she exerts is always pure and elevating, and thus ennobles those most intimately connected with her, give the Gen my warm thanks for his kindness to my dear Sister tho' I know her to be entirely worthy of any attention bestowed upon her.[5]

Like Martha, Lydia never married. In the fall of 1866, she was thirty.

By the spring of 1868, Scott had distanced himself from Martha. What had happened? "Why was promise not kept?" she had asked her diary the previous October, in tiny writing at the bottom of the page. She had seen Scott that day, just four days after she returned south for the new school year.[6]

She asked him once what had happened.

Is one who made so many promises and pledges my friend still? she asked. She thought of him by day and dreamt of him by night, his absence rendering her heart "a dead lifeless thing." As she waited for a response, the pain of suspense seemed a physical thing. When his reply came, it wasn't the message she had been hoping for.[7]

I never forget my old friends, though circumstances may separate for a while — I don't forget the claims I am under. He would never come to see her again, she realized. Perhaps it was too painful for

---

5 Lydia Schofield to MS, Nov. 25, 1866.

6 MS diary, Oct. 31, 27, 1867.

7 MS diary, Mar. 12, 1868.

him to see her, even to think of her, as it was for her. "If I cannot be remembered without pain," she reasoned, "better to be absent from mind." The thought consoled her some.[8]

In the classic feminist text *Reading the Romance*, Janice Radway argued that romance novels are structured essentially to reconcile women to patriarchy. Men behave strangely, erratically, distantly throughout these texts, tossing the female protagonist into painful emotional turmoil. But there is a reason for this, the story promises: he acts this way only because he loves her. Martha never read Radway, but she read *Jane Eyre*. If ever I forget the distance between us, I remind myself that she found Jane's relationship with Mr. Rochester romantic.

* * *

Later, when Martha couldn't sleep at night, she stayed up and reread copies of their letters. "The originals long since burned," she wrote. The lack of an agent rankles my historian's brain. Accidentally burned? Or *were* burned? It wouldn't have been the first time she burned letters better kept private. In any event, he seems to have left even less of a record of their relationship than she did. According to the archivist who compiled his collection, "the papers could perhaps be useful in shedding light upon the Reconstruction Era in South Carolina. However, there is virtually no revealing personal correspondence." This may have been intentional. A history of Henry County, Ohio, written during Scott's lifetime offered a caveat: "These pages do not contain the space required for a detailed narrative of the events of the life of this man, nor is it in accord with his desire that such detail should be given." Gosh, I wonder why. Scant information about *his* personal life.[9]

8 MS diary, Mar. 22, 12, 1868.
9 Schofield to Polly, Jan. 19, 1913; "Robert Kingston Scott: An Inventory

The general was in many ways a good man – a ferocious defender of the Union and, later, the rights of freed people. An active supporter of the women's suffrage movement. But his nearly impeccable politics did not translate into an understanding that the way he treated the women in his life was also political.

* * *

Martha's closest friend at this time was fellow teacher Mary Taylor, with whom she lived. The two often shared a bed, dreamily reading passages of *Little Women* and similar books to each other, imagining themselves as the characters. In the spring of 1869, Martha and Mary read *Rebecca; or, a Woman's Secret* by Caroline Fairfield Corbin. It had been a gift from Eliza, who had worked for months to find a copy for her sister, eventually special-ordering it from the book's Chicago publisher. Part of Eliza wanted to refrain from giving Martha the book until she could do so in person so she could witness her sister's pleasure in reading it. "I know thee will like it," she predicted, "there are so many beautiful sentiments; so many heart experiences, so much deep, inner life of woman, that woman can best appreciate and understand ... Dear precious sister! How thy own life would stand on an equal with that of 'Reba' could its nobleness its silent uncomplaining pain, its sacrifices and its triumphs be written." Reba, mistreated by one man, loved by another.[10]

(It *can* be written, Eliza, though perhaps it will not look the way you would have liked. I have no interest in silent,

---

of His Papers in the Ohio Historical Society," 1969), Ohio Historical Society, Columbus, OH; Lewis Cass Aldrich, ed., *History of Henry and Fulton Counties, Ohio, with Illustrations and Biographical Sketches of Some of Its Prominent Men and Pioneers* (Syracuse, NY: D. Mason & Co., 1888), 606.
10 Eliza Schofield to MS, Mar. 1869.

uncomplaining pain. If Martha could not scream her pain, I will scream it for her.)

Under normal circumstances, Eliza would have been right: Martha would have adored the book, and she would have appreciated the comparison to such an unselfish character. After all, Beth was her favorite of the March sisters. "Dear Beth," she wrote of the doomed young woman, "she was the sweet flower that was transplanted to a Higher Home I wish my life had been as pure, for it may not be long − ." She felt herself too much like Jo, too quick to anger, too hasty-tempered.[11]

Instead she could barely read it, stumbling as she read aloud to Mary over words of love and marriage and motherhood as woman's highest calling. Martha believed this too, and she knew she would never have this life. Mary moved closer to her friend and clasped her hand, knowing she must comfort her but not knowing why.

* * *

When Sadie got engaged at the end of 1868, Martha wept in Mary's arms. Mary herself got engaged just a few months later, on March 11, 1869. Major William Stone, another Freedmen's Bureau, was a *very* good man − perhaps, in his personal life, all that the general could not be: open, available, and steadfast. A self-professed devotee of sentiment, his whole heart belonged to Mary. In certain ways, theirs was a shadow version of Martha's relationship with the general.

Rather more accurately, it was the other way around.

Martha's approval was important to Stone. "I hope you'll not think Mary has been hasty or unwise in the step she has taken," he wrote to her, "I hope you'll not be induced to bring

---

11 MS diary, June 6, May 30, 1869.

an action ~~of~~ for grand larceny against me for 'taking, stealing and carrying away' Mary's heart! If you do, I shall plead to the jurisdiction of any court before which you might bring me." He even asked her for marriage advice, "which your profession of teacher renders you competent to give!"[12]

March 11 was no ordinary day for Martha either: it was the day that, the previous year, she had asked the general if he was still her friend. She cut a few lines out of her diary that day in 1869 but otherwise insisted that she was all right. "I think I am resigned to the past, satisfied with the present – and do not <u>dread</u> the future – ."[13]

But when she learned the date of Mary's engagement, a different truth emerged. Stone's letter may have arrived before Mary had a chance to tell her friend of the news (though Stone, as he made sure to tell Martha, had urged his new fiancée to do so as soon as possible), but it was from Mary that Martha learned the date. In late April, Mary told Martha the story of her engagement. Martha's initial elation quickly turned to despair. "She showed me – a handsome plain gold ring dear dear girl I was wishing her all happiness – when the date – <u>March</u> 11th – shot a great pain through my heart – Why, oh! God – why do such <u>little</u> things still give me pain – am I never, never to get over – the sorrowful past – ."[14]

Martha didn't do an especially good job hiding her reaction to Mary's engagement. It seemed to Mary that Martha didn't love her, that she was, perhaps, incapable of loving anyone. But she didn't know. Martha had shared her despair over Sadie's engagement, but she had told Mary nothing about her relationship with the governor.

Only months later, as she prepared to return north for the summer, did Martha confide any of this to Mary. The

---

12 William Stone to MS, Apr. 4, 1869.

13 MS diary, Mar. 11, 1869.

14 MS diary, Apr. 26, 1869.

Crosshatch

night before Mary and the major left for Charleston, Martha sat downstairs late into the night, hoping that Mary might join her so that she could unburden herself to her friend in person. Instead she put her feelings into a letter, along with strict instructions that Mary not read it until she had left Aiken. It broke Mary's heart to know "that thee has <u>loved, as I know thee can love</u>. and has had to give all up – and live along with out it."[15]

But still, but still.

> *Darling, thee won't blame me –*
> Mary's love had worked out.
> *If I ask just once more –*
> Couldn't Martha's, too?
> *Must it be forever? Is there no hope, that you will yet come together?*
> If the general were everything Martha said he was?
> *Thee writes as if he was so good – so I feel that it must be so some times.*

But then, that was the whole problem, wasn't it?

Martha's last recorded meeting with the general took place days after she confided in Mary. It was the end of the school year, and she was staying in a hotel in Columbia, South Carolina, before traveling north. She wrote him a note asking him to come see her that afternoon. "He came round and staid one hour – It was distant, unsatisfactory – & short – but I rejoiced that I had <u>this</u> much – for I left with no bitter feelings – ." She left for Philadelphia later that day. She received a letter from "R. K. S." that November, but as far as I can tell they never saw each other again.[16]

That did not mean she stopped thinking about him.

There was the 1913 letter to her niece Polly, in which she

15 Mary Taylor to MS, June 27, 1869.
16 MS diary, June 26, Nov. 20, 1869.

recounted the details of the general's visit in 1866, one of at least three times she did so in the last decade of her life.

There was a poem, written around the same time, in which she imagined reuniting with him after her death, hearing again the words he said to her on that day. He had been gone for nearly a decade at that point. So many of the people closest to her were gone.

> I can close my eyes –
> and see the open
> door to Eternity –
> There stands my father
> & my mother and
> My sisters Lydia Sarah & Eliza
> to welcome me – and
> behind them the
> strong noble man
> who after their greeting,
> opens his arms re-
> -peating the words
> of long ago – lord
> made my soul for
> yours & yours for mine
> for all eternity –
> 45 years of waiting – [17]

There was a memory. "The Lord writes on faces," a visitor to the school told her in 1910, "he has written on yours." Again she returned to that day – the kid gloves, the old sofa – wondering if the general had seen such writing in her face then, "the face he so loved – that was not even pretty." Again she remembered their closeness, their chasteness, the trouble and expense he had gone to. The fact that a part of her had left

17 Poem, 1910 [1913].

Crosshatch

with him that day, never to return. "No wonder time seems long waiting for the re-union in the – promised land," she wrote.[18]

Three years before her death, she was still lonely. I imagine she died that way too, which breaks my heart. I can't let her story end here.

---

18 Memories, n.d.

Epilogue

"Why a biography of M.S.?" Katherine Smedley, Martha's biographer, once asked. "M.S. interesting because she lived intensely – Her feelings were deep and real and worth studying." Surely many people lived their lives this way, many more than those for whom we have evidence. What made Martha different was that she shared those feelings.[1]

Until she didn't. Here is where I run into the same problem that so many historians of women have faced: after age thirty, she did not write about her personal life.

Martha had many reasons for ending her diary at the end of 1869, at which point she had kept it for twelve years. Sadie's engagement and marriage had broken her heart. Her dear friend Mary Taylor also wed that year, which reminded Martha of her own romantic disappointments.

She was also so very busy, so very tired. "I am sorry now to give it up – but – I have much writing to do – and it tires me – so that this seems the one thing I can leave out of an almost exhausted life."[2]

At the end of the year, a violation of her privacy may also have soured her on recording her innermost thoughts and feelings. In early December, she briefly returned to the

---

1 Katherine Smedley notes, n.d.
2 MS diary, Jan. 1, 1870.

house during the school day to find her diary out on the table. Someone had been to her room, rummaged through the secret door in Martha's desk, and, assuming that Martha would not be home until later, neglected to return the materials. The meddling angered Martha.

But 1869 was also the year that she turned thirty. It was not a happy event for her. "The day has been so full of memories – many sad ones – ," she wrote, reflecting on her life, "I fear there has been many many errors, and little to be proud of – ... and sitting here, in the stillness, mine seems like a broken wasted life."[3]

In the end, her age was the biggest reason why she gave up her diary. At thirty, it had become clear to her that her life would not follow a conventional trajectory; it would not include marriage or motherhood, and so her diaries would not serve the purpose she had once envisioned. "<u>Once</u> I had hoped these books would <u>amuse</u>, my grandchildren," she wrote, but "now I feel that <u>Motherhood</u> – . that most glorious of all the Fathers Blessings – will not be given to me – . I am a woman – and all woman hope for this – But I accept my life as God wills it – and so – loosing <u>this</u> – will be content with less – ."[4]

For twelve years she had barely missed a day, except for those times when she was very sick. But on New Year's Day in 1870, she determined that "this Diary will now only be a partial broken record – of Events." She could still record events in her notebook, but it would no longer be a journal – a crucial distinction. She could not imagine writing her personal thoughts and feelings without a frame, without a reason that existed outside of herself.[5]

I've had to chart her life in different ways from this point

---

3 MS diary, Feb. 1, 1869.
4 MS diary, Feb. 1, 1869.
5 MS diary, Jan. 1, 1870.

Crosshatch

forward. Luckily, she didn't disappear from the historical record, though her presence there is very different. She spoke the truth about all of the writing she had to do: about suffrage, about the school, about racial terrorism. Rather than mostly writing for and about herself, she mostly wrote for others. Rather than writing primarily about her feelings, she primarily wrote about politics. Perhaps, as writer Mary Patterson speculated, "the whole story [of her own life] didn't seem very important to her."[6]

A century later, in 1969, Carol Hanisch wrote and distributed "The Personal Is Political," a classic second-wave feminist text. In it, she defended the new consciousness-raising groups of the women's liberation movement, in which small groups of women discussed their personal experiences. To their detractors, men and women alike trained by the male-dominated white Left to believe that only grand theories of capitalism and imperialism were worth discussing, these meetings were solipsistic and apolitical, mere distractions from the "real" issues.

Hanisch disagreed. For how long had women been told to distrust their experiences and emotions? For how long had others rejected the truth of those experiences and emotions? "It is at this point a political action to tell it like it is, to say what I really believe about my life instead of what I've always been told to say," she argued.[7]

At the very heart of this ethos was the belief that personal experiences and emotions were worth talking about. I believe this, and Martha did too, once, whether she realized it or not. But I have trouble applying it to my own life, and so I'm trying to do it for her, instead.

---

6 Patterson, *Servant of the Least*, 3.

7 Carol Hanisch, "The Personal Is Political," Feb. 1969, online at http://www.carolhanisch.org/CHwritings/PIP.html.

Christina Larocco

***

Early critics did not know what to make of poet Adrienne Rich's classic feminist text *Of Woman Born*. They found it odd: the way it includes "personal testimony mingled with research, and theory which derived from both." But to Rich, this approach is part of the point. "It seemed impossible from the first to write a book of this kind without being often auto-biographical, without often saying 'I,'" Rich writes, "Yet for many months *I buried my head in historical research and analysis in order to delay or prepare the way for the plunge into areas of my own life which were painful and problematical*, yet from the heart of which this book has come. I believe increasingly that only the willingness to share private and sometimes painful experience can enable women to create a collective description of the world which will be truly ours." Later, when trying to write about her mother, she reveals to the reader that "*a folder lies open beside me as I start to write, spilling out references and quotations, all relevant probably, but none of which can help me to begin.*" The emphasis is mine, those words where I feel she is speaking directly to me. I always write about myself last, once my individual experience has been contextualized and justified.[8]

Rich's text provides some of the backbone for Carolyn G. Heilbrun's equally classic feminist text *Writing a Woman's Life*. The great tragedy of women's lives, Heilbrun argues, is *storylessness* – the inability to imagine, to live, to write one's life, by which she means, I think, one's narrative trajectory. As both individuals and as artists, then, women must imagine, claim, and record their experiences. The process of doing so, as Heilbrun imagines it, is mutually constitutive: "Women come to writing," she argues, "simultaneously with self-creation." In order find their stories, women must first believe that such

8 Adrienne Rich, *Of Woman Born: Motherhood as Experience and Institution* (1976; repr., New York: W. W. Norton and Company, 1995), ebook.

240

Crosshatch

lives can be lived, and they cannot do so until such stories have been written. We understand our lives through the stories that are available to us. New lives produce new stories, and new stories facilitate new lives.[9]

I drank these words up when first I encountered them, for they seemed so similar to what I am trying to do here. But there's a caveat. For Heilbrun, "woman's selfhood, the right to her own story, depends upon" what literary scholar Myra Jehlen calls her "ability to act in the public domain." Accomplishment, achievement, agency. I've grown frustrated with this version of feminism. I understand where it came from and why it's important. But it's not enough anymore.[10]

Perhaps this frustration, ultimately, is why I'm obsessed with narrative − the way we construct it, the way we use it to make sense out of our lives − but fundamentally dislike it, why I have no interest in reading or writing it. Hewing to male models of achievement, the hero's journey and so forth, may make a narrative, but it is not the only way to make a life. In truth, whose life, no matter their gender, really looks like this?

* * *

I had drafted this entire epilogue before I realized that, in writing about Martha's decision to stop writing about herself, I had included *nothing* about myself. Why, if the personal is indeed political, should I not? Is it that my life is made up of nothing but what Virginia Woolf calls non-being − those parts of life that are nothing but foggy, staticky boredom? Who wants to − who *can* − write about that? Emily Dickinson managed somehow to marshal the considerable resources of her inner life to write quietude. But if Woolf couldn't, I certainly

9 Carolyn G. Heilbrun, *Writing a Woman's Life* (New York: Ballantine Books, 1988), 117.
10 Jehlen quoted in Heilbrun, *Writing a Woman's Life*, 17.

can't. Writing with a purple pen, as she did, isn't enough to make me the writer she was.

It's mostly by choice, of course, that my life has been like this. I could have had adventures. But I'm a good girl, whose misadventures were largely restricted to a very few years in the late 1990s and early 2000s; a stay-at-home girl, whose life gets smaller with every choice I make.

The whole point, or one of the points, of this project is that women's lives, especially the internal part, the small, secret parts we keep in our hearts, are worth writing about. Did I design an entire book, complete with a subject who is a lot like me but different enough that I wouldn't see it until years later, to convince myself of this fact? Different enough that I could pretend that, in writing about Martha, I wasn't actually writing about myself? I wanted to write memoir but couldn't, so I wrangled Martha to write one with me, to provide those stories, those experiences, that I could not. Because she lived an actual *life*.

In certain ways I have used Martha as my I-then, someone whose actions I can look back and reflect on. Because if I were only to look back and reflect on my own experiences, what would there be to say? I have so few. I am a writer of personal narratives who can't or won't write about herself. Friends and colleagues push me: "Where are *you* in this?" Digging through a box of old papers recently, I even found this comment from my eighth-grade English teacher. But my insides needed to be hidden even more than did the acne that I shellacked with makeup.

This is no way to produce meaningful writing.

As I neared the end of this project, I started to think about what I wanted to write next. Sometimes I fantasized about a middle-grade girl detective story, or the dystopian screenplay that I started in 1998 and never finished, which failure I can only now attribute to a case of ADHD that went undiagnosed

Crosshatch

for decades. It's too bad because I could have been ahead of the curve on that one. But my next book will probably be another quasi- or non-memoir, autobiography disguised as scholarship (as, perhaps, all scholarship is), something that starts out personal but that my brain abstracts until it doesn't even feel like it's about me anymore — and thus feels like it's okay to write about. Bring in enough postmodern theorists and nothing feels personal anymore.

I once tried to wrangle Alex to write a memoir with me.

"I only have two stories!" I told her half-jokingly, "Being in New York on 9/11 and our relationship! That's it!" I even have a whole structure figured out: we'll each write passages — memories, reflections, scenes — then respond to the other's sections. I still need another person, or another subject, to give my life structure and meaning, to give it *story*. I don't know how to talk about myself in an unmediated way, without a frame or a justification. In that way, I suppose, I am like Martha. On some level, I believe that women must bury their selves in others in order to justify writing about themselves.

Narrative means change, story theorists tell us, and the story necessarily ends when change does. For Martha's sake, for my sake, I wish this weren't so. Because what else is there to say? What exists beyond story?

I guess, as Lorrie Moore says, it's just, like, life.

* * *

When I was young I had so much to say, to write. Thoughts, feelings, desires, fears flowed out of me. I could not stop. I wrote all day long, journaling or writing poetry instead of paying attention in school. I worked on my screenplay late into the night. No matter what the genre, I was always writing about myself, myself, myself, always writing from the depths of my teenage despair. But I fear I have nothing left to say.

One hundred years before "the personal is political" entered mainstream discourse, Martha's writing about feminism and about her personal life were almost entirely separate. She provides no model of how to combine these things. This was true when she was young, and it became even clearer as she got older. But there was so much of value to record in her life after thirty. Has "the personal is political" taken into consideration women's experiences – and the value thereof – as they age?

What does thirty mean in a woman's life these days, anyway? Not much, really. I spent my thirtieth birthday, in 2011, wearing an ugly Christmas sweater and a tiara and getting drunk with my cousins, passing around an ancient bottle of champagne on my aunt and uncle's back porch. I ask this question about women's personal writing now as a woman in her forties, a woman entering middle age.

"What do you think Martha would say if she knew you were writing about her?" Josh asked me once. I thought for a moment before responding. She wouldn't approve of me in many ways, not because of how feminism has changed the way we live but because I am sometimes materialistic, frequently vain, often loud. The thought of sitting silently in meeting makes my skin crawl. But these concerns, I think, would be secondary.

"I think she'd wonder why," I told him. "I don't think she thought her life was worth writing about."

* * *

February 14, 1868 was cold and snowy in Boston, so different from what Martha faced in South Carolina. But Louisa May Alcott, at thirty-five, six years older than Martha, was a kindred spirit. Louisa was just months away from beginning

Crosshatch

to write *Little Women*, eking out a living with stories she wrote under a pseudonym, wishing she could send more money to her family.

She was in a foul mood when she returned to her flat from running errands as the thin winter sun set. At her doorstep, she found Mr. B., a literary agent who had a proposition for her: Would she write "one column of Advice to Young Women"? He handed her a $100 bill, a sum for which she would have agreed to write anything, including a Greek oration.[11]

The finished piece hit much closer to home. "It was about old maids," Louisa recorded in her diary. "'Happy Women' was the title, and I put in my list all the busy, useful, independent spinsters I know, for liberty is a better husband than love to many of us."

Far from unfortunate, spinsters represented a "class ... of superior women." They found purpose in medicine, in teaching, in ministering to the poor. And they did it happily, cheerfully, never complaining about their personal circumstances or women's political lot. There was far too much work to be done to leave any time for that. "My sisters," she implored her readers, "don't be afraid of the words, 'old maid,' for it is in your power to make this a term of honor, not reproach."[12]

Martha could have been one of the women about whom she wrote, a paragon of the educated, useful single woman. "Modern Spinster," Martha once joked that her initials stood for. It was not what she would have chosen for herself. But she had purpose, she had family and friends and students who loved her. Perhaps she would have found some consolation in her fellow single woman's words – but if so, she didn't write

---

11 Louisa May Alcott diary, Feb. 14, 1868, in *Louisa May Alcott: Her Life, Letters, and Journals*, ed. Ednah D. Cheney (Boston: Little, Brown, and Company, 1919), 197.

12 Louisa May Alcott, "Happy Women," in *Alternative Alcott*, ed. Elaine Showalter (New Brunswick, NJ: Rutgers University Press, 1988), 203, 205.

about it.[13]

Louisa thought about the article as she ate her supper, a squash pie that earlier had fallen in the snow, and wrote it with the money sitting in front of her. She "went to bed a happy millionaire, to dream of flannel petticoats for my blessed Mother, paper for Father, a new dress for May, and sleds for the boys."[14]

* * *

The Greta Gerwig version of *Little Women* made me cry, not as much as the Winona Ryder version that I watched over and over again as a girl, but enough that I wasn't ready to talk about it until after the credits rolled. In the car, I explained to Josh what Jo means to girls and women who envision a different kind of life for themselves, more and different possibilities for moving through the world as a woman.

"In the end, she does kind of want what other people have," he pointed out. "Does that bother you?" In the scene he referred to, Jo confesses her loneliness to Marmie.

It didn't bother me, though. I'm glad Jo wants both, and I'm glad we get to see her wanting both. Martha wanted both, too. Her longing for both love and political equality, for both convention and revolution, brings me back to the original goal of this project: excavating women's personal, not just public, lives.

* * *

As a child, I never wanted to read *Little Women*. I thought it would be boring – the same reason that Alcott did not want to write it. "I don't enjoy this sort of thing," she confided to her

13 MS diary, Feb. 20, 1866.
14 Alcott diary, Feb. 14, 1868, in Cheney, *Louisa May Alcott*, 197.

Crosshatch

journal early in the writing process, "Never liked girls or knew many, except my sisters; but our queer plays and experiences may prove interesting, though I doubt it." Halfway through the first volume, she seemed to receive confirmation of her fears. Mr. Niles, her publisher, "thought it *dull*; so do I." But young girls in a test audience found it delightful. *Little Women* isn't boring, of course, though I confess that even as an adult I prefer the movie versions.[15]

Alcott famously did not want Jo, her protagonist, to marry. I understand why this was so when she wrote. If marriage was not only one of the few real options available to women in real life but also the *only* way a woman-centered narrative could have a happy ending, then *not* ending with marriage – showing that there were other options, other ways to be happy – was subversive, something the radical Alcott must have wanted dearly.

"Above all else," Gillian Brockell writes in the *Washington Post*, "Louisa May Alcott was a radical. From an early age, she was an abolitionist. She was also a feminist, committed to never marrying, and loved to pull up her skirts and go for a long run through the woods. Alcott's most famous work, *Little Women*, was nearly the opposite – a light, juvenile novel focused on sisterly love and domestic peace. And though it was semi-autobiographical, she hated it."[16]

I can't entirely agree with this. It is a mistake to dismiss *Little Women* as Alcott did – as conservative, unimportant, *boring*. What could be more radical than insisting on the importance of young women's voices and longings?

All of their longings.

Even Alcott seemed to recognize this function of the book to some extent, often in less frequently quoted passages from

---

15 Alcott diary, May and June 1868, in Cheney, *Louisa May Alcott*, 198–99.
16 Gillian Brockell, "Girls Adored Little Women. Louisa May Alcott Did Not." *Washington Post*, Dec. 25, 2019.

her diary. She was surprised at how well the first volume turned out. It was "not a bit sensational, but simple and true, for we really lived most of it; and if it succeeds that will be the reason for it." Readers "seem to find friends by their truth to life, as I hoped." Young women saw their own lives reflected in Alcott's words. How rare that must have been. How sad, how maddening, that Louisa's life was the one deemed unacceptable, the only sister whose story diverged so fundamentally from her fictional counterpart.[17]

It's easy, then, to see Alcott's (coerced) decision to marry Jo off as a betrayal of both women's feminism. Letters poured in from passionate readers demanding to know whom the sisters married and insisting that Jo marry Laurie, her best friend and next-door neighbor. "Girls write to ask who the little women marry," Alcott wrote in her journal, irritation palpable, "as if that was the only end and aim of a woman's life. I *won't* marry Jo to Laurie to please any one." She didn't, and it was the right decision. Though as a girl it was painful to see Winona Ryder turn down Christian Bale, what adult woman wouldn't prefer youngish Gabriel Byrne? That wasn't Alcott's point, of course.[18]

Gerwig's *Little Women* has been hailed as a corrective that restores the story Alcott originally wanted to write. But Gerwig's great trick is not, as critics have suggested, to make Jo more like Alcott, but the even more daring feminist feat of melding the two. How easy it would have been to let Jo remain unmarried, to let her write great literature unburdened by a spouse. But Gerwig lets Jo want romance, too. For this decision among many reasons, I feel she is a kindred spirit.

"If the main character's a girl," the editor Mr. Dashwood (Tracy Letts) tells Jo (Saoirse Ronan) at the beginning of the

---

17 Alcott diary, Aug. 26, Oct. 30, 1868, in Cheney, *Louisa May Alcott*, 199, 201.

18 Alcott diary, Nov. 1, 1868, in Cheney, *Louisa May Alcott*, 201.

Crosshatch

2019 film, "make sure she's married by the end. Or dead. Either way." It's a nod and a wink to what twenty-first century viewers know not only about how the March sisters ended up but about how and why Alcott steered them there. Later, Dashwood balks at Jo's insistence that her protagonist not marry either of her love interests. Why, the writer version of Jo asks, should her namesake marry when she has spent the entire book insisting she will not? It is, she tells him, the wrong ending.

She's right, of course. It's difficult to see Jo's romance with Friedrich, who disappears for such long stretches of the story, as anything other than tacked on (Alcott, that scamp, invented him just to thwart her readers' expectations). In part this is because it seems strange to see a character as obviously queer as Jo dropped into a heteronormative relationship. I imagine that every college theater performance of *Little Women* plays with this aspect of her character. But it's also true that Jo spends much of the book insisting she will never marry. "I don't believe I shall ever marry," she tells Laurie in declining his marriage proposal, "I'm happy as I am, and love my liberty too well to be in a hurry to give it up for any mortal man." She resigns herself to the life of "a literary spinster, with a pen for a spouse, a family of stories for children, and twenty years hence a morsel of fame." Film adaptations have followed Alcott's lead; both the 1994 and 2019 versions maintain Jo's dialogue in the proposal scene.

But Jo is lonely. Beth, her favorite sister, is dead, and Meg and Amy have gone away to start their own families. "You are right in one thing," she tells Marmee in the book, "I am lonely." This scene provides the emotional climax to the 2019 film. Jo wants to be loved. "I'm so sick of people just saying that love is all a woman is fit for," she begins, echoing Alcott, "But I'm – I'm so lonely." The catch in Ronan's voice makes me ache.

And why shouldn't she be lonely? Why shouldn't she want love? I want Jo to be more than a writer, more than her external accomplishments. I want her to be a person. Gerwig figures out a way to let her be both – not by ignoring the original text, but by recognizing its nuances in ways previous filmmakers have not.

Gerwig's final intervention addresses what is and is not worth writing about. Toward the end of the film, Meg (Emma Watson) and Amy (Florence Pugh) ask Jo about her writing. "I started something, but I don't think it's very good … It's just about our little life," Jo responds. "Who will be interested in a story of domestic struggles and joys? It doesn't have any real importance." "I think it is probably quite boring," she tells Mr. Dashwood when she sends him the first several chapters. Amy disagrees: "Maybe it doesn't seem important because people don't write about them … Writing them will make them more important."

Tell women's stories. Tell them, tell them, tell them. Tell them until people believe in their importance.

Little Women ends with Jo at thirty, the same age that Martha was when she stopped writing about herself, the same year that she realized she, like Alcott and unlike Jo, would never marry. In a sense, Alcott stopped writing about herself between parts one and two of *Little Women*. That was when her life ceased to be enough. It could have been within months of Martha making the same decision in February 1869. At thirty-six, Louisa was just a little older.

Alcott wrote sequels to *Little Women*, many of them beloved. But it must have been a harder task once Jo's life diverged so fundamentally from hers. Alcott possessed a heartier soul than I, but perhaps she wondered, as she grew older: why wasn't her actual life worth writing about? One hundred and fifty years later, the task is left to writers, to biographers, to filmmakers.

To me.

ACKNOWLEDGMENTS

Thank you to the team at Blackwater Press, especially Elizabeth Ford.

Thank you to everyone who read and commented on all or part of this book, including Karen Beattie, Ashley Bethard, Barbara Lanciers, Ashley Lopez, Jon Malesic, Janna Maron, Dyan Neary, Anne Helen Petersen, Emilly Prado, Alexa Vallejo, Elissa Washuta, Martha Wolfe, and Vonetta Young. I apologize if this list excludes anyone.

Thank you to VQR and Tin House for the opportunity to attend workshops in 2017 and 2019, respectively.

Thank you to the Friends Historical Library of Swarthmore College, which provided funding that helped make this work possible, and to the archivists and other staff members at the Friends Historical Library.

Thank you to Josh Landow, whom I endeavor every day to deserve.

Thank you to my family, which has retained its resilience amid loss.